GCSE PSYCHOLOGY
A STUDY GUIDE

GCSE PSYCHOLOGY
A STUDY GUIDE

Jean McNiff and Mike Stanley

Hyde Publications

© Jean McNiff and Mike Stanley

All rights reserved. No reproduction, copy or transmission of any part of this work may be made without written permission from the publisher.

First Edition 1994

Published by Hyde Publications
57, Exeter Road, Bournemouth,
Dorset, BH2 5AF, UK

ISBN 1-874154-12-0

Printed and Bound by
Bourne Press Limited, Bournemouth

Contents

	Page
Acknowledgements	vi
Introduction	vii

PART ONE   GCSE PSYCHOLOGY WITH THE NEAB 1

PART TWO   UNITS FOR STUDY

Personal processes

Unit 1	Human development and the nature-nurture debate	17
Unit 2	Perception - how it happens	22
Unit 3	Perception - the nature nurture debate	33
Unit 4	Learning - behaviourist approaches	41
Unit 5	Learning - cognitive and ethological approaches	53
Unit 6	Memory - what is it and how does it work?	61
Unit 7	Remembering and forgetting	70
Unit 8	Emotion - physiological foundations	77
Unit 9	Emotion - arousal and stress	85
Unit 10	Language	94
Unit 11	Thinking, problem solving and intelligence	104
Unit 12	Attention	112
Unit 13	Sleep, dreaming and states of consciousness	119
Unit 14	Intellectual and moral development	127

Interpersonal Processes

Unit 15	Attachment and separation	137
Unit 16	Gender and socialisation	146
Unit 17	Social perception	153
Unit 18	Stereotyping and prejudice	159
Unit 19	Social influence	166
Unit 20	Group pressures	175

PART THREE WORKED PAPERS

| Examples of papers and mark schemes | 183 |
| Specimen papers and mark schemes | 200 |

| Index | 219 |

ACKNOWLEDGEMENTS

We wish to thank Mike Cardwell, Richard Gross, Nicky Hayes and Paul Humphreys for their painstaking reading of the text in draft form, and for their very helpful comments. Their continued support is very much appreciated.

We acknowledge with gratitude permission from the NEAB to reproduce the specimen examination material in Part Three.

We wish to thank our publisher, Alan Hyde, for his enduring patience and good humour in supporting our project.

Introduction

Welcome to this Study Guide. We hope it will be really useful for you in your studies.

The Guide is for three different student audiences, and is also intended as teacher resource material.

The first audience is students who are studying for the NEAB GCSE Psychology examination. The new syllabus will be in operation in 1996, and this Guide gives detailed advice on the new syllabus, the kinds of examination questions that will be set, and the marking schemes that will be used. You will find advice about the new syllabus in Part One of the book, and you will find worked examples of sample material and specimen papers in Part Three. This is really useful material, and will be an invaluable guide in your studies.

The second audience is students who are studying for syllabuses other than the NEAB. The centre section of study units will be particularly useful for you, because it gives notes, revision exercises, 'Need to know' and summary sections on all major topics on psychology syllabuses. The specimen examination material in Part Three will also be invaluable in testing your knowledge of psychology.

The third audience is students who are studying on post-GCSE courses, or courses in the social sciences. The Study Guide provides a general foundation course, in quick reference form. The summaries and 'Need to know' sections will be of particular value for you, as they indicate the major areas of study involved in any Psychology syllabus.

As well as being a quick, easy and comprehensive study guide for students, this book is intended to help busy teachers in preparing and delivering lessons. The graded exercises that accompany each section provide useful resource material for written and oral self-study assignments. The exercises are presented in a variety of formats and levels of difficulty, so that they may be tackled by students at any level.

Another really useful feature is the last section in each unit on Suggestions for Coursework. For each topic, there are several suggestions about the kind of coursework that might be undertaken in relation to that topic. For students on post-GCSE courses, there are suggestions about coursework of a more challenging nature. These will provide useful hints about the kinds of projects that you might undertake for your more advanced studies.

Structure of the book

The book is divided into three parts.

Part One gives detailed and comprehensive guidance about the new NEAB syllabus, coming into effect in 1996.

Part Two provides study units on each topic set for the NEAB syllabus, as well as units covering other general topics in psychology. These would include topics contained in the GCSE syllabuses of the other two major Examining Boards, SEG and MEG. Each unit has study notes on basic issues, evaluations of these notes, a summary, a 'Need to know' section, and student exercises - structured questions, written exercises, topics for discussion, and suggestions for coursework. All of these may be undertaken as classroom-based work or self-study material.

Part Three gives comprehensive worked examples of the kind of examination questions that will be set from 1996 onwards, indicating how the new two-tier system will work. This section is followed by the specimen papers that are issued by the NEAB, again with advice and guidance on type of examination question and the marking schemes used.

We hope you will find using the book both useful and fun. We have enjoyed putting it together. We know that there is currently no other book available that provides the kind of guidance you will find here, and we are looking forward to using the book in our own classrooms.

Feedback is always much appreciated. If you would like to comment on the book in any way, or suggest ways in which it might be improved, please contact us in care of Hyde Publications, 57 Exeter Road, Bournemouth, Dorset BH2 5AF, UK. We would be very pleased to hear from you.

We wish you great enjoyment and success in your studies.

Jean McNiff and Mike Stanley

Part One
GCSE Psychology with the NEAB

A syllabus with flexibility

All GCSE courses are designed with the needs of sixteen year olds in mind. However, the NEAB Psychology syllabus also reflects the interests and experience of mature students. This means that the course should appeal to a wide range of students including adults following part-time or distance learning courses.

The syllabus conforms to the GCSE Criteria for Social Sciences as prescribed by the National Curriculum, and the standards required for the award of grades will be the same as for the GCSE in general.

Background to the new syllabus

From 1996 onwards, the GCSE examination in Psychology will take a new form. Therefore, as early as September 1994, course structures in many centres will need to be modified to accommodate syllabus changes.

In order to conform with the Social Sciences Criteria, two main areas needed to be taken into account in the revision of the old syllabus. These were the subject content and the terminal examination.

Subject content

In the new syllabus there is more emphasis on the biological theories of behaviour. Apart from this, the topics covered are essentially the same as in the old syllabus. However, the new syllabus is more specific about the areas of Psychology which need to be covered and, because of major changes in the terminal examination, schemes of work will require some modification.

Terminal examination

From 1996, there will be two tiers of assessment, and grades will be awarded across levels which range from A* to G. The two tiers organisation is a requirement of the Criteria mentioned above. Therefore the new syllabus contains two options offering overlapping ranges of grades:

Option P - Grades C to G

Option Q - Grades A* to D

One outcome of this change will be to stretch the most able candidates whilst ensuring that the syllabus is accessible to students with a wide range of ability. The scheme of assessment is designed to give everyone the opportunity to demonstrate what they know, understand and can do.

All Psychology students will write one externally set and marked written examination paper which will carry 80% of the total marks. The other 20% is for coursework. Therefore, you will write an examination either for Option **P** or for Option **Q**. You will not be allowed to write for both options.

Your teacher will discuss with you which option you should enter, and the grade you are expected to reach should lie within the range of target grades for that option. It is very important that you are entered for the right option. Try to guard against unreasonable expectations. This is particularly important advice for Option **Q** because over-ambitious students could end up without a grade if their answers have not reached grade D standard. There is a certain amount of safeguard here, however, because, in practice, papers could also provide evidence of attainment one grade below the targeted range in Option **Q** and one grade above in Option **P**. Therefore, it will be possible in certain circumstances to earn grade E on Option **Q** and grade B on Option **P**.

If your teacher's estimate of your expected grade coincides with the overlap in grades of the two options, i.e. grades D and C, your entry will be determined by the amount of confidence your teacher has in your achieving that grade.

The written paper

For Option **P** and Option **Q** all questions will be compulsory. Both papers will be written at the same time (another reason why you cannot be entered for both!), and some questions or parts of questions may be common to both papers. However, in Option **Q** the examination is longer:

Option **P** - 2 hours
Option **Q** - $2^{1}/_{2}$ hours

The papers for both options will comprise both short-answer and structured questions and each paper will contain two sections, Section A and Section B. Section A will include methodology questions and Section B will include structured questions and stimulus questions based on material such as advertisements, pictures and newspaper articles.

Option **P** candidates are advised to spend thirty minutes on Section A and ninety minutes on Section B. Option **Q** candidates are advised to spend forty minutes on Section A and one hour and fifty minutes on Section B. There will be opportunities for extended prose writing in each paper.

The main difference between the two options is that in Option **Q** there will be greater emphasis on the assessment of candidates' understanding of the wider implications of the subject material and of the candidates' ability to evaluate, interpret and critically analyse the knowledge and understanding acquired. There will be more opportunities for extended prose answers in this option.

In order to achieve the correct balance of marks between Section A and Section B in both options, this is what you can expect to see in the examination:

Option P

Section A	Two methodology questions of 15 marks each
Section B	Structured questions with a total of 60 marks (the number of questions in this section may vary from year to year)
Total marks	90 (80% of your grade)
Time	120 minutes

Option Q

Section A	Two methodology questions of 20 marks each
Section B	Structured questions with a total of 70 marks (the number of questions in this section may vary from year to year)
Total marks	110 (80% of your grade)
Time	150 minutes

The A* grade

From 1994 onwards, examination boards are required to identify candidates at the top end of the A grade who will be awarded an A* grade. This is determined by a simple mathematical calculation, rather than any subjective assessment of the quality of candidates' work. The number of students qualifying for the A* grade will depend on the width of both the grade A and grade B bands in any given year. The percentage of all candidates falling into this category will therefore vary from year to year but it could be in the region of 2%. Therefore, if you do not achieve this grade you should not be disappointed, even if you have been top of your class throughout the course. Fewer than 100 students achieved this in Psychology in 1994 out of a total entry in excess of 5000.

Grades A to G (differentiation)

The scheme of assessment has been designed to give all candidates the opportunity to demonstrate what they know, understand and can do. The question papers for both options will make use of different subject content and question formats to test your knowledge and skills in a variety of ways and to enable the awards for all candidates to be based on positive achievement. Mark schemes make provision for rewarding all answers which have merit, and will thus ensure that all questions are accessible to all candidates. Therefore differentiation is achieved by outcome in each option.

Spelling, punctuation and grammar assessment (SPG)

In all GCSE subjects, including Psychology, marking criteria for accurate spelling, punctuation and grammar will apply to all components of the examination (both coursework and the written examination). 5% of the marks available will be allocated to these skills. Examiners deal with this by adding an appropriate number of marks to those you have already earned in your written work. Marks are never deducted for poor spelling, so don't worry about that. In an examination system that relies on 'positive marking', you will never be penalised in that way. Don't be afraid to write more just because you are unsure of correct spellings. The additional information that you give will probably be worth more than the mark that may not be added because of inaccurate spelling.

What mark do I need to pass Psychology?

This is not a closely guarded secret. However, it is not possible to give an exact mark for each grade - this will vary from year to year depending on how difficult the examination is judged to be. Contrary to popular myth, standards at GCSE level are not falling. The same standard is maintained from year to year by committees who compare the performance of this year's students with the performance of those who were examined last year. The difficulty of the examination will vary over the years quite naturally, which means that, to achieve the same standard for any grade, you may have to earn more or fewer marks than candidates earned in the previous year for the same grades.

Each year the Examination Board publishes a report on the examination after all the grades have been awarded. It contains very useful information from examiners about how students responded to every question in the examination paper, pointing to the strengths and weaknesses shown by candidates. This report is available to all centres and it is well worth having a look at it in preparation for your own examination.

The examiners' report also contains information about the mark ranges for the award of grades. This will help you to find out roughly how many marks you need for each grade. There are no guarantees here, but based on statistics gathered over the last few years, candidates who achieved 75% of the marks available (including coursework) earned an A grade. Those who exceeded 50% were awarded at least a grade C. However, it must be pointed out that these figures are based on the old syllabus and we must look to the 1996 examiners' report for the first indication of the grade boundaries for the new syllabus. The important thing to remember is that the same standard will be carried across to the new examination.

Bearing this in mind, however, it is interesting to see how these marks can be accumulated looking at the assessment objectives contained in the syllabus. You should look at the syllabus for a detailed breakdown of these but a summary is given below.

Assessment objectives

A large proportion of marks (70% of the total available in the written paper and coursework) is for 'knowledge and understanding'. Therefore you certainly need to have accurate knowledge and understanding of facts, studies and issues in Psychology. This includes Psychology and its applications to everyday life as well as the ethical issues in the practice of Psychology.

The other 30% of marks will be for 'analysis and evaluation'. These are high level skills which demonstrate, amongst other things, your ability to interpret and use information, and to draw conclusions. This will be particularly important to you if you are entered for Option **Q**.

How different are the two options?

It has already been mentioned that the length of the terminal examination is different in the two options and that in Option **Q** there will be more opportunities for extended prose in your answers. Nevertheless, the two options contain the same subject areas and this means that teaching groups could easily contain students who will be entered for Option **P** and students who will be entered for Option **Q**.

The syllabus is divided into three broad subject areas which are then sub-divided into topics:

1 Individual processes
    (a) Perception
    (b) Learning
    (c) Memory
    (d) Emotion

2 Interpersonal Processes
    (a) Development of social behaviour
    (b) Social perception
    (c) Social influence

3 Methods of Investigation

In the syllabus, the subject content is displayed in a two-column format. Material which will be assessed in the terminal examination for Option **Q** only is given in the right-hand column. This material is an expansion of material given in the left-hand column for Options **P** and **Q**. Material in the left-hand column for Options **P** and **Q** may be assessed on the papers for both options but candidates for Option **Q** will be given opportunities to demonstrate higher levels of attainment and an ability to evaluate, interpret and critically analyse the knowledge and understanding acquired. The exception to this is Section 3 (Methods of Investigation) which is not presented in two columns. This is because the section comprises a listing of those methods and techniques which are necessary for the proper study of the topics in the other two sections and therefore will be taught to all candidates at appropriate places throughout the course.

Here is an example of how one topic is presented in the syllabus using the two-column format and how it might be examined in both Option **P** and Option **Q** (including a typical mark scheme used by examiners):

PERCEPTION

Options P and Q	**Option Q**
Perception as an active process illustrated by:	The organisation, translation and reconstruction of sensory information:
the difference between sensation and perception;	perception as a modelling process: Gregory's theory of cues and hypotheses;
the distinction between the proximal stimulus and the percept;	size constancy and explanations of the distortions of perceived size, distance and movement;
2D images and 3D percepts illustrated by ambiguous figures and simple illusions;	
distance perception: the relevance of depth cues; everyday examples of distortions and perceived size, distance and movement.	
Structures and functioning of the eye: with particular reference to the formation of a sharp retinal image.	Description of the visual pathways leading to the visual cortex.

Factors affecting perception: motivation, perceptual set, emotion, previous experience, context, instructions, reward, deprivation, perceptual defence/sensitisation and attention on visual perception.

The ability to discuss these factors in terms of applications to examples in everyday life.

Option P: Example of a 10 mark structured question

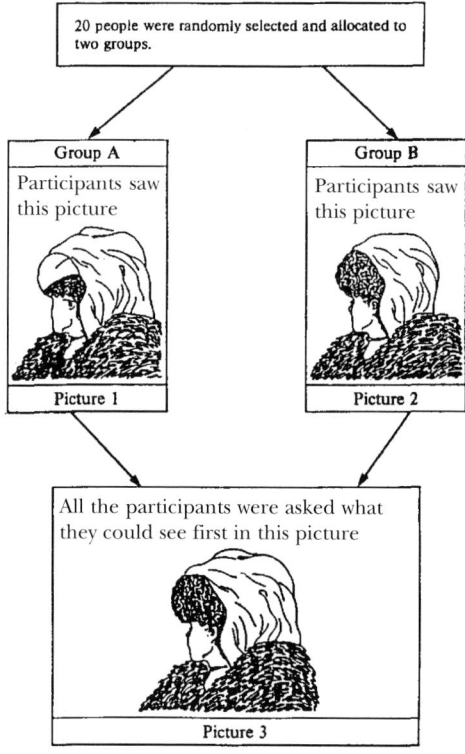

(a) What do you think the majority of Group A participants said they saw when they first saw picture 3?
....
....(1)
(b) What does this study tell us about the difference between sensation and perception?
....
....(3)
(c) Describe one study which shows that perception is influenced by emotion and motivation.
....
....
....(3)

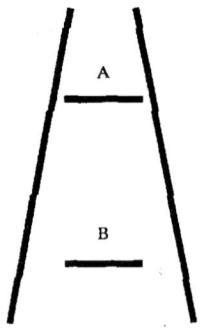

(d) Name one monocular depth cue to be found in the above illusion.

....
....(1)

(e) What does the illusion that line A is longer than line B tell us about perception?

....
....(2)

Option P: Example of mark scheme

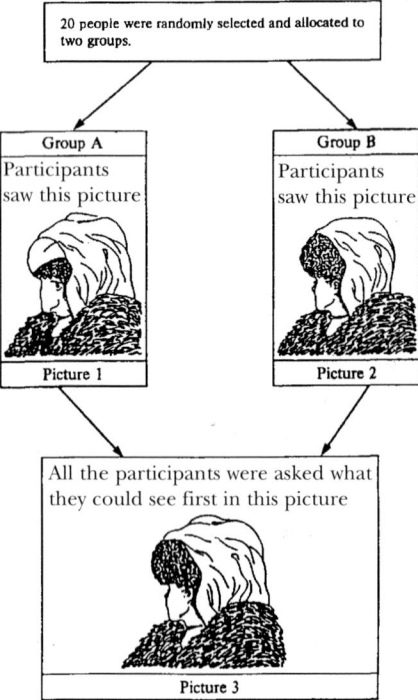

(a) What do you think the majority of Group A participants said they saw when they first saw picture 3?

..............OLD WOMAN...............(award 1 mark) ....

(b) What does this study tell us about the difference between sensation and perception?

.... EVERYONE SENSED ....(award 1 mark for this idea) ....

.... THE SAME PICTURE ....(award 1 mark) ....

.... BUT PERCEIVED IT DIFFERENTLY ...(award 1 mark) ....(3)

(c) Describe one study which shows that perception is influenced by emotion and motivation.

..........ACCURATE METHOD ...... (2 marks) .... BASIC METHOD (1 mark).

.........ACCURATE RESULTS.......(1mark) ....

....

....(3)

(d) Name one monocular depth cue to be found in the above illusion.

.... ANY CORRECT RESPONSE .... (award 1 mark) .... (1)

(e) What does the illusion that line A is longer than line B tell us about perception?

.........ANY REFERENCE TO ACTIVE INTERPRETATION ... (award 1 mark)..

.... OF SENSATION.......(award 1 mark) .... (2)

Option Q: Example of a 15 mark structured question

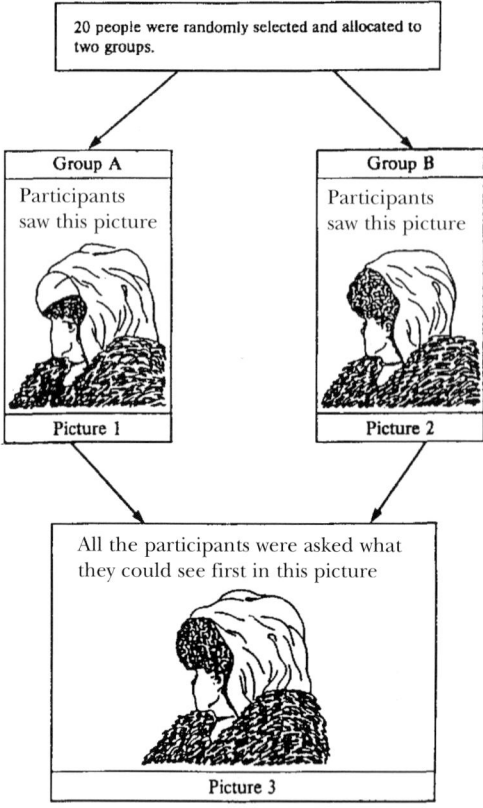

(a) What do you think the majority of group A participants said they saw when they first saw picture 3?
....
....
....(1)

(b) What does this study tell us about perception?
....
....
....(3)

(c) Describe and evaluate one study which shows that perception is influenced by emotion or motivation.
....
....
....(5)

Advice on the new examination papers 11

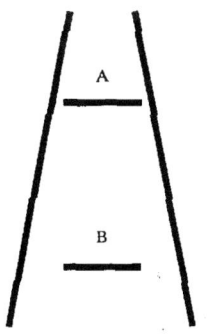

(d) Name one monocular depth cue to be found in the above illusion.

....
....
....(1)

(e) How have psychologists used the theory of size constancy to explain the illusion that line A seems to be longer than line B?

....
....
....(5)

Option Q: Example of mark scheme

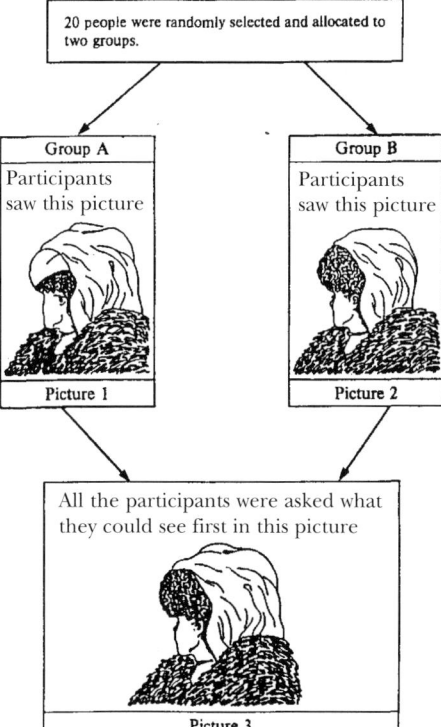

(a) What do you think the majority of group A participants said they saw when they first saw picture 3?

..............OLD WOMAN..............(award 1 mark)..(1)

(b) What does this study tell us about perception?

................ACTIVE PROCESS...

.....................INTERPRETATION OF SENSATIONS...

BASED ON PREVIOUS EXPERIENCE...................................REFERENCE TO

PERCEPTUAL SET....................(any 3 for1 mark each - max. 3 marks)..............(3)

(c) Describe and evaluate one study which shows that perception is influenced by emotion or motivation.

..... ACCURATE METHOD ...... (2 marks) or BASIC METHOD ... (1 mark) ....

.... DIFFERENCE .... (1 mark)...and

DIRECTION....................................(1 mark)..

EVALUATIVE COMMENT ..... (1 mark) ....(5)

(d) Name one monocular depth cue to be found in the above illusion.

............ANY CORRECT CUE..........(1 mark)..(1)

(e) How have psychologists used the theory of size constancy to explain the illusion that line A seems to be longer than line B?

.... DEPTH CUE AROUND A .... (1 mark) .... CAUSES PERCEPTUAL

SYSTEM TO INTERPRET .... (1 mark)......... A TO BE FURTHER AWAY THAN B ... (1 mark) ... HENCE IT SCALES UP THE PERCEPTUAL SIZE .... (1 mark) ... TO COMPENSATE FOR THE ASSUMED SMALLER RETINAL IMAGE ... (1 mark) and 1 mark for any of the following correctly used: .... ACTIVE PROCESS, MODELLING HYPOTHESES (max. 5 marks) ....(5)

NOTE: *Notice the flexibility of the mark scheme to allow a range of responses and a choice of relevant studies. Marks can be accumulated in a number of ways.*

Assessment of practical and experimental skills

Practical work is an essential part of the course and will count for 20% of your GCSE grade. Coursework requirements for the new syllabus have not changed. Your project folder should contain evidence of 40 practical skills which will be assessed by your teacher during the course and then moderated externally by a member of the Examining Board.

Detailed guidance on how to conduct and present coursework is contained in the companion book to this one, entitled ***GCSE Psychology Coursework: A Practical Guide*** by Jean McNiff and Mike Stanley, and published by Hyde Publications.

Part Two

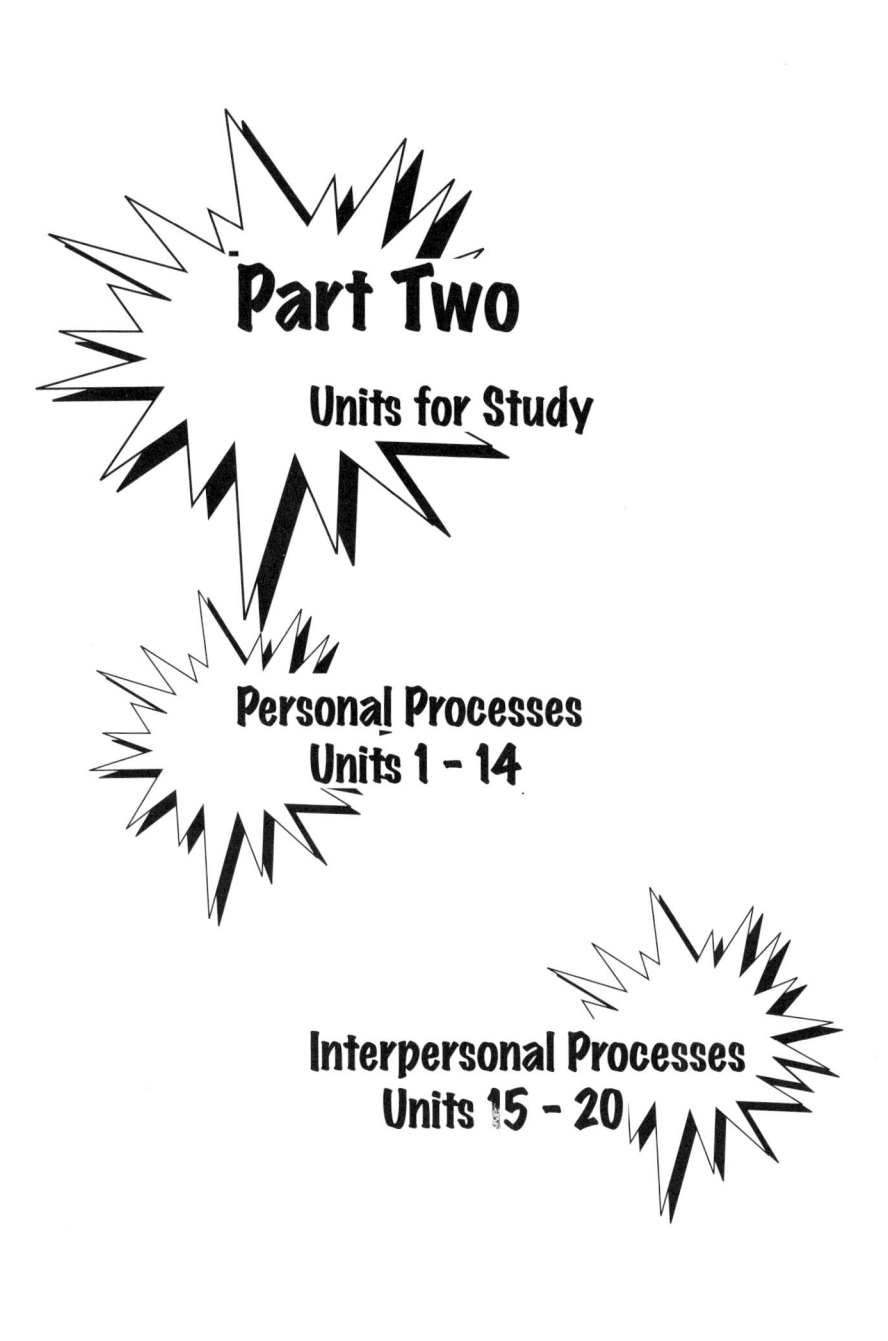

Units for Study

Personal Processes
Units 1 – 14

Interpersonal Processes
Units 15 – 20

Unit One
Human development and the nature-nurture debate

This unit deals with the question

How have I become the person that I am?

There are two main points of view here - the empiricists and the nativists. Their opinions are opposite each other. There are also the interactionists who are in between.

This unit looks at the nature-nurture debate, which runs through most of psychology.

The main themes for this topic are

1 How do humans and non-human animals develop?
2 What are the main factors that influence development?
3 How far is behaviour inherited or learned?
4 What are the implications of these views?

1 How do humans and non-human animals develop?

The name given to the process of becoming mature is **maturation**. It is all about developing as fully as possible.

It seems clear that physiological development in humans and non-human animals follows a straightforward pattern. We go through different physiological stages of growth in the same order and at roughly the same time of life.

Other non-physiological aspects of human development are not so straightforward. It is impossible to say exactly how we develop, and whether we develop as a result of natural processes, or whether we learn to develop in some ways. These questions have been investigated for a long time, and a debate has grown up around the questions, which is called the **nature-nurture debate**. There are two main sides in this debate: the **empiricists** and the **nativists.** The **interactionists** have a middle viewpoint.

Empiricism

Empiricists believe that we are born as a 'blank slate', and that development happens as a result of outside influences. This is the nurture side of the debate, and it says that I grow into the person I am because of the environment, including other people. I have learned to behave and think in the way that I do, and I have learned to become a particular kind of person. Psychologists who think like this are called empiricists. They are sometimes called environmentalists, although this term is also used nowadays to mean someone who cares for the environment, so stick with the word 'empiricist'.

An example of an empiricist is ***Watson***, who said that he could turn a child into any kind of person he chose.

Nativism

Nativists believe that we are born 'pre-programmed' with all mental capacities. Development is a natural process and happens as a result of inheritance, that is, through our genes and biological makeup. This process is known as **genetic transmission**. Things like intelligence, personality and perception are inborn.

An example of a nativist is ***Gesell***, who said that children needed the right conditions to help them develop as they were supposed to.

These are both fairly extreme views. There is a more balanced view.

Interactionism

Interactionists believe that development depends on genetic and environmental factors working in harmony.

An example of an interactionist is ***Hebb***, who said that, for instance, an egg developed naturally but depended on the right conditions for its survival and growth.

2 What are the main factors that influence development?

Empiricists believe that the most important factors are the right kind of external stimuli. If some aspects of behaviour are learned, it is important that the right kind of stimuli and models are available for people to learn from.

Nativists believe that the most important factors are the right kind of conditions that will encourage development to go on naturally. If some aspects of behaviour are innate, they need to be encouraged and protected.

Interactionists believe that a mix of both the right kind of stimuli and good environmental conditions are necessary for growth.

3 What are the implications of these views?

These views go right through the whole of psychological and scientific enquiry.

Empiricists believe that things like memory, intelligence, learning, and social behaviour in general are things which may be studied, manipulated and measured. The aim of psychology is to explain how development happens in order to predict and control it.

Nativists believe that these things happen of their own accord, and are processes which may be studied. The aim of psychology is to explain how development happens in order to understand and improve it.

Interactionists believe that these things happen naturally but with a little help from their friends. The aim of psychology is to explain how development happens in order to keep it going.

4 Evaluation

Psychologists sometimes take an extreme position as empiricists or nativists. This can lead to very lively discussions. You must make up your own mind about these things, but, whatever opinion you have, you must always back it up with solid evidence from your own experience and from what you have studied.

One of the most exciting things about psychology is that there are no definite answers. Often, students begin a course expecting to find all the answers. Instead, they just find more questions to which there are still no answers. Everything in psychology, and in science in general, is provisional - that is, it is always open to a better argument. Don't feel confused because there are no absolute answers. Learn to think for yourself. Read the work and come to your own conclusions. You are a researcher yourself, and you have every right to have your own opinion about things - provided you can back it up with evidence!

5 Summary

Empiricists believe that we are born without any kinds of pre-programming. We develop entirely because of the environment, including other people. **Watson** is an example of an empiricist.

Nativists believe that we are mentally pre-programmed and that development happens naturally, as long as the right conditions are provided for development. *Gesell* is an example of a nativist.

Interactionists believe that development is a mixture of inherited factors and interaction with the environment. *Hebb* is an example of an interactionist.

6 Now ⟹ Over to you . . . .

1 *Fill in the missing words*

Empiricists believe that we are born as a b............ s............, and develop b............ of the e......................
Nativists believe that we are born 'pre-programmed' and develop as long as the right c........................ are provided.
Interactionists believe that development is a m.................... of inherited factors and the e................................

2 *Choose the correct name*

An example of an empiricist is Watson/Gesell/Hebb.
An example of a nativist is Watson/Gesell/Hebb.
An example of an interactionist is Watson/Gesell/Hebb.

7  Written exercises

1 What are the main differences between empiricists, nativists and interactionists?
2 Where do you see these differences in psychology?
3 Why is it difficult to reach any definite conclusion about ideas to do with nature or nurture?

8   Topics for discussion

1. What do you think about the nature-nurture debate, particularly as it applies to personality and intelligence? Are those things inherited or learned?

2. What do you think about the views of Watson, Gesell and Hebb?

3. Do you think psychological development can be measured in the same way as physiological development - that is, can we measure, say, the growth of intelligence in the same way that we can measure the growth of our body?

9 Need to know

☞ Can you explain the difference between empiricism, nativism and interactionism?
☞ Can you give an evaluation of each?
☞ Can you name all the psychologists in this unit, and give a description of their point of view?
☞ Can you say how the nature-nurture debate runs right through psychology?

10 Suggestions for coursework

It is unlikely that you would undertake any coursework to do with this topic by itself, but it is very likely that you will do some coursework where the nature-nurture debate is important. Doing your coursework is a very good way to understand what the topics of psychology are all about, as well as to learn about the methods of scientific investigation. Coursework can be really interesting to do, and reinforces your own image as an independent researcher. Good luck!

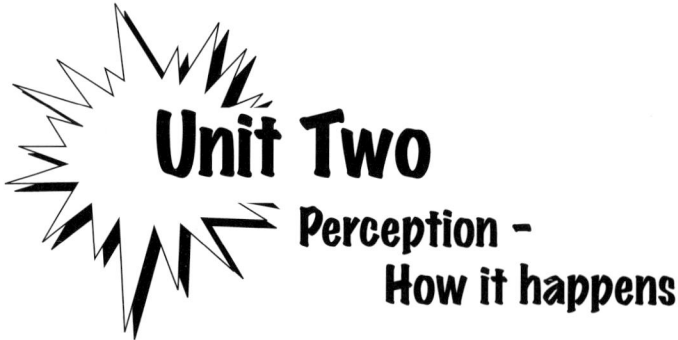

Unit Two
Perception – How it happens

This unit deals with the question

How does perception happen?

There is a big difference between sensation and perception. A handy way of remembering the difference is this:

visual sensation: I look with my eyes -
   i.e. I see the visual field
visual perception: I see with my brain -
   i.e. I interpret what I see

The interesting question now is, How is it that we are able to perceive at all? How is it that our visual field is all on a flat surface - we see a 2-D picture - yet we perceive whatever we see as 3-D objects existing in space?

There are five factors which help us understand. They are

1 the difference between sensation and perception
2 depth cues which help perception
3 other operating principles which help perception
4 perception as an active process
5 factors affecting perception

This unit is about visual perception, which is where most work on perception has been carried out. Perception refers to the other senses as well - taste, touch, hearing and smell. Perception in hearing is dealt with in Unit 4, Selective Attention.

1 Sensation and perception

Sensation is a physiological process, and perception is a cognitive process. Sensation is the reaction of our sense organs to external stimuli. We see shapes and colours, and we hear noises, for example, without necessarily giving them meaning.

> **Remember** Perception is the interpretation of the information we receive through our senses.

Examples

sensation	perception
- hearing a loud noise - seeing a blue colour overhead - feeling a sweet taste on the tongue and prickles in the nose	- interpreting this as the door slamming - interpreting this as the sky - drinking lemonade

Psychologists tend to agree about what sensation is. It is a physiological response to stimuli in the environment. The problem arises when we ask how it is that we turn our sensations into perceptions. How do we convert the hearing of a loud noise into a door slamming? How do we make sense of our contacts with the environment?

Sometimes our perceptions mislead us. Try putting your very cold hands into hot water. You might not immediately perceive the water as hot. Or go into a dark room after being in the bright sunshine outside. You will see shapes, but you will need time to interpret these as real objects and perceive them for what they really are.

Look at this.

What do you see? You see a 2-dimensional figure. What do you perceive? You perceive a 3-dimensional scene. Amazing, isn't it? How does it happen?

Psychologists have tried to find answers based on the evidence from their studies. Here are some of the factors which they believe are important in helping us to make sense of the things around us.

2 Depth cues which help perception

Depth cues help us to give objects distance, and turn them from 2-D images into 3-D percepts.

There are (a) **monocular depth cues** - i.e. cues using one eye only;
          (b) **binocular depth cues** - i.e. cues using both eyes.

The **principle of constancy** is also relevant here.

Monocular cues

There are 7 of these:

☆ **Relative size** Objects which are far away produce a smaller retinal image than objects which are near (remember the Ames room).

☆ **Height in plane** Objects which are far away are higher in the visual field than objects which are near. These tend to be lower in plane.

☆ **Light and shadow** Light usually falls on things from above, so we use this to tell us which way up things are. Shadows also usually fall to the side, so this helps us judge distance.

☆ **Perspective** Objects which are farther away appear smaller and closer together than objects which are near. This helps us judge distance and depth. Parallel lines going away into the distance (such as railway tracks) appear to come closer together.

☆ **Superposition** When on object obscures the view of another, we tend to think of it as being in front of the other, or overlapping it.

☆ **Gradient of texture** Objects farther away are smoother; objects near are coarser. Think of the pebbles on a beach.

☆ **Motion parallax** When we are moving, objects farther away seem to move more slowly than objects which are near. This helps us to judge distance. A jet plane travelling at 600 mph appears to crawl across the sky, whilst a car passing you at 60 mph seems to whizz by.

Quick tip

Remember these cues - **R, H in P, L&S, P, S, G of T, Mp** - by using the mnemonic **Risking Headaches in Planes, Lecturers and Students Play Silly Games of Testing Migraine Pills,** or make up a mnemonic of your own.

Binocular cues

☆ **Convergence** The eyes converge; we go 'cross-eyed'. This helps us to judge distance.

☆ **Disparity** Objects appear to occupy a different space depending on which eye we use. This also helps us to judge distance.

Quick Tip

Remember these cues - **CD** - by using the mnemonic **'Compact Disc'** or make up a mnemonic of your own.

3 Other operating principles which help perception

☆ **Constancy**   This means that we perceive an object to be the same, even though we have different images of it. Joe seen far away (small) and Joe seen near (large) is still perceived as the same size (size constancy). A cup seen with its handle to the side and later with its handle to the front is still seen as the same cup (shape constancy). My red car seen in neon lighting is still perceived as a red car, even though the lighting makes it seem orange (colour constancy).

☆ **Environmental factors**

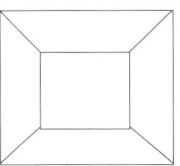

Annis and Frost (1973) carried out investigations into how our environment affects how we perceive things. They discovered that most Westerners operate in terms of a **'carpentered environment',** because our surroundings are largely manufactured and have lots of straight lines and angles, so we would expect to see things in straight lines and angles. People living in natural habitats such as jungles could have some difficulty in perceiving straight lines and angles if they had never lived in a carpentered environment.

4 Perception as an active process

> Perception is the interpretation of the information we receive through our senses.

The eyes see and the brain interprets. The brain can offer only one interpretation at a time - e.g. we see only one version of the Necker cube at any one time, even though there are two possible interpretations (it is an example of an ambiguous figure).

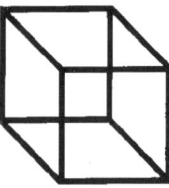

The Gestalt (pronounced 'gshtalt'; 'Gestalt' = 'form' or 'pattern' in German) psychologists said that we inherit mental processes that give order to what we see. In other words, our ways of perceiving are innate, and they develop in a 'natural' way. These are called the **Laws of Prägnanz**, or principles of organisation.

Principles of organisation

There are four of these:

☆ **Figure-ground effect** When we look at Rubin's vase we see either figure (vase) or ground (faces). We cannot see both together.

☆ **The principle of similarity** Items which are similar tend to be grouped together.

```
        XOXO              XXXX
        XOXO              OOOO
        XOXO              XXXX
        XOXO              OOOO
```

    We see 4 columns   We see 4 rows

☆ **The principle of proximity** Items which are near each other tend to be grouped together.

```
        OOOO   X X X X X   OOOO   X X X X
```

We tend to see the O's as grouped together rather than the X's because the O's are near each other, but the X's are spaced.

☆ **The principle of closure** We tend to 'finish off' images that are unfinished. We perceive

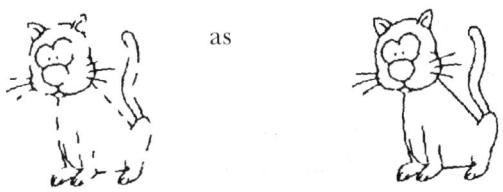

as

Remember these cues by using the mnemonic '**Funny girl Sue is a perfect comic**' or make up a mnemonic of your own.

5 Factors affecting perception

There are a number of factors which can affect how we perceive things. These involve

motivation, perceptual set, emotion, previous experience, context, instructions, reward, deprivation, perceptual defence/sensitisation, attention.

These factors are dealt with in the relevant units in this book.

Perceptual set may be seen as a separate factor. On the other hand, it may be seen as incorporating a number of the factors already listed. The idea of perceptual set is generally to do with how ready we are to perceive and the expectations we have which influence how we perceive things.

Perceptual set

The idea of **set** is '*how ready we are*'. The most common aspects involved in set are

☆ **Expectation** - we tend to see/hear what we expect to see/hear. *Bruner and Minturn* (1955) tested people to see whether they saw an ambiguous figure as a letter B or the number 13.

☆ **Primacy effect** - we tend to see/hear a whole in terms of how we saw/heard the first elements. *Jones* (1968) asked people to judge how intelligent problem-solvers were through watching the way they worked. Those who did well on the first elements of the problems were seen as more intelligent.

☆ **Motivation** - how much we want to perceive influences how and what we perceive. *Gilchrist and Nesburg* (1952) suggested that people would perceive pictures of food as brighter and tastier when they were hungry.

☆ **Emotion** - state of emotion influences how and what we perceive. ***Solley and Haigh*** (1958) found that children's drawings of Santa Claus were much bigger in the run up to Christmas than in the days afterwards. ***Erikson*** (1951) found that aggressive people interpreted pictures as showing violent scenes, but non-aggressive individuals saw them as harmless.

☆ **Values** - the kinds of attitudes we hold in general influence the way that we see things. ***Postman, Bruner and McGuiness*** (1946) investigated people's reactions to taboo words, and suggested that they put up a **perceptual defence** to unpleasant stimuli.

6 Evaluation

These are all very interesting studies, and give us clear empirical evidence that something happens in the brain to help us perceive what we see. However, no one has yet given a satisfactory answer about what exactly does happen. It is still a mystery what actually happens in the brain to help us convert a flat 2-D retinal image into a meaningful 3-D image.

In post-GCSE work you will read the work of ***Gregory, Gibson*** and ***Marr***, who all offer theories to explain what might happen when we turn sensation into perception - i.e. when we move from seeing to perceiving. There is, however, no definite answer.

7 Summary   How does perception happen?

How we see and what we see depends on several factors including:

1 Depth cues which help perception
    Monocular depth cues: relative size, height in plane, light and shadow, perspective, superposition, gradient of texture, motion parallax.
    Binocular depth cues: convergence, disparity.
    Constancy: size, shape and colour constancy.

2 Principles of organisation (Laws of Prägnanz)
    Principles: figure-ground, similarity, proximity, closure.

3 Perceptual set
    This includes: expectation, primacy effect, motivation, emotion, values.

8 Now ➔ Over to you...

Fill in the missing words in questions 1-4

1 The difference between sensation and perception is that sensation is
....
while perception is..
....

2 Depth cues which help perception are called

(a) m.................. depth cues which may be seen with .... eye.
(b) b.................. depth cues which may be seen with .... eyes.

3 Monocular depth cues are
        R................................
        H.............................. in P............................
        L............................ and S.........................
        P................................
        S................................
        G............................ of T..........................
        M............................ P..............................

 Binocular depth cues are
        C............................
        D............................

4 The Principles of Organisation are

    (a) ....
    (b) ....
    (c) ....
    (d) ....

5 *Only one of the statements below is correct. Which one is it?*

Perceptual set refers to   (a) whether we can perceive;
                               (b) whether we are ready to perceive;
                               (c) whether we are wearing glasses or not.

9 Written exercises

1 Explain the difference between sensation and perception. Give at least three examples from your own experience to show the difference clearly.
2 What is quite remarkable about perception? Why does perception puzzle psychologists?
3 What is the importance of depth cues?
4 What is the difference between monocular depth cues and binocular depth cues?
5 Name all the depth cues you know. Say what their function is.
6 Explain size constancy, shape constancy and colour constancy. Give two examples of each from your own everyday experience.
7 What did the Gestalt psychologists believe?
8 What principles of organisation (Laws of Prägnanz) did the Gestalt psychologists formulate?
9 What do we mean by perceptual set? Give two examples from your everyday experience that shows how perceptual set operates.
10 Describe the studies of Bruner and Minturn; Jones; Gilchrist and Nesburg; Solley and Haigh; Erikson; Postman, Bruner and McGuiness.

10 Topics for discussion

1 Explain what the difference is between sensation and perception, and say how psychologists think we might be able to show how 2-D images can be turned into 3-D percepts. Use examples from your own everyday experience.

2 From your immediate surroundings, such as your classroom, living room, etc., say which depth cues you can identify, and say how they help you to perceive the world as existing in three dimensions.

3 Say how the Principles of Organisation help us to organise what we see into meaningful images.

11 Need to know

- Can you explain what depth cues are?
- Can you name all the depth cues, and say which are monocular and which are binocular? What is the function of the two different types?

▷ Can you name all the Gestalt Laws of Organisation? Can you give everyday examples of how they operate?

▷ Can you describe some of the factors involved in perceptual set, and give everyday examples of how they operate?

▷ Can you name all the psychologists mentioned in this unit, and describe their work?

12 Suggestions for coursework

1 Try to replicate the studies of Bruner and Minturn, or Gilchrist and Nesburg, or Solley and Haigh. Use your imagination to adapt the studies to your situation and resources; for example, you could ask children to draw pictures of Easter eggs instead of Santa Claus, if you are doing the project during the month of March.

2 Investigate the effect of the size of the fin angle on the apparent extent of the Müller-Lyer illusion.

3 Investigate the effects of depth cues by lining up objects side by side with

    (a)   both eyes open
    (b)   one eye open

More challenging studies

1 Carry out a survey/questionnaire study to test perceptual ability with regard to depth cues, or the principles of organisation. Give a group of people a series of pictures which contain a number of these cues, such as a tree in the foreground and a sun in the sky. Vary your cues in the series of pictures. Ask your participants questions about the cues: 'Which features of Picture A are closest to you?'; 'Which features of Picture D are farthest away?' Count the number of answers they give. Draw some conclusions about the usefulness of depth cues.

2 Carry out an investigation into the features of perceptual set. Test familiarity/meaningfulness effect in this way. Ask two groups to do a simple task, such as writing a letter, or reading, or typing - something routine, but which occupies their attention. Tell them in advance that you will be saying certain things to them at intervals, but that they should pay no attention to you.

    With one group, every thirty seconds or so, quietly say an odd word. Note and time their reaction. Occasionally insert the name of one of the people in the group. Note and time the reaction of this person. Is there any difference in the reaction of this person from that of the other people?

    With the other group, tell them that you are going to be saying the names of fruit occasionally. Every thirty seconds or so, quietly say an odd word. Note and time their reaction. Occasionally insert the name of a fruit. Note and time their reaction. Is the reaction time any different?

2 Carry out an experiment to test the features of perceptual set. Organise two groups (independent samples design). Tell Group A that they are going to hear certain sounds, such as bleeping sounds, among others, and that they should indicate, perhaps by tapping the table, as soon as they hear the sound. Play previously tape-recorded sounds, including bleeping sounds, for a minute or so. Note and time the reaction of each participant to the various sounds. Is there a difference in reaction time to bleeping sounds and to other sounds? Do the same with Group B, only tell them that they are simply going to hear a series of sounds. If there is a significant difference in response time to the indentified sound, you could argue that expectation is a factor in perceptual set.

3 Investigate the perceptual skills of children and adults and compare them. Ask a group of children to draw a picture of their immediate visual field within environment X - perhaps a classroom, or your living room. Ask a group of adults to do the same thing, also in environment X (independent samples design). Tally how many instances of the laws of organisation and depth cues you can find in the pictures. From your results, what conclusions can you draw about the development of perceptual skills as people mature?

Unit Three
Perception – the nature-nurture debate

This unit deals with the question

How do we come to have our perceptual abilities?

Perception means 'making sense of things around us'. Do we learn to perceive through experience? Are our perceptual skills learned? This is an empiricist view. Or are we born with these skills? Do we come to perceive as a natural process, as the nativists believe? There is no one, definite answer, although there are many studies that try to show that one view is better than the other.

Most studies have been done on visual perception, and some on auditory (hearing) perception. Remember the difference between perception and sensation. Sensation is a physiological process, whereas perception is a cognitive process. We can say that we sense with our senses, but we perceive with our brain.

The main themes for this topic are

1. What is the difference between sensation and perception?
2. Is perception learned or inborn (the nurture vs. nature points of view)? How does perception develop?
3. What evidence is there to support the empiricist, the nativist and the interactionist views?

1 Sensation and perception

In Unit 2 we saw that there was a difference between sensation and perception. Sensation is a physiological response to stimuli which come to us via our senses. Perception is a process of the brain which helps us to interpret what we sense, and turn it into meaningful ideas. There is as yet no definite answer about how this happens, and how we make sense of the things around us.

A big question is whether perception is learned or innate. Do we learn how to make sense? Do we learn to make sense through a slow process of adapting to our environment, or trial and error, or other ways? Or do we automatically begin to perceive things? Is perception just one of those things that develops, part of the natural growth systems of the body? This is part of the nature-nurture debate, and the two sides of the argument are as follows.

2 How does perception develop?

Empiricists say that perception develops as a result of our interactions with the environment. We actively learn to perceive. We do not learn to see, hear, taste, smell or feel. These are inherited characteristics. But we have to learn how to give meaning to the information that we are receiving through the senses. We learn how to do this. This is the nurture side of the debate.

Nativists say that perception develops naturally as we grow. It is just one of many 'normal' things, such as memory and intelligence, that we inherit as part of our biological make-up, and that matures over time. Nativists think that perception develops regardless of environment or external stimuli. This is the nature side of the debate.

3 Evidence

Psychologists have tried to find answers based on the evidence from their studies. There are many studies in the literature, and some of them are grouped here to show you the different kinds of approaches that psychologists take. These are the studies that you need to know for your GCSE course.

1 Perceptual adaptation or readjustment studies

Stratton (1983) designed a pair of spectacles that turned the world upside down. He wore them for a week. After the first few days the inverted world appeared normal.

Köhler (1962) wore goggles with tinted lenses. One half of each lens was green and the other half red. When he took them off after a few hours he 'saw' everything coloured the opposite way to the lenses.

Hess (1956) fitted prisms over the eyes of chickens which shifted the image to the right or left. The chickens never succeeded in adapting. They always missed the grain they were pecking at.

> **Evaluation**
> These studies suggest that adult humans (Hess, of course, worked with chickens) seem able to learn to see things differently and adapt to new situations, but the studies do not throw any light on whether perception is innate or learned.

2 Human cataract patient studies

Von Senden (1960) studied a group of people who had regained their sight after a cataract operation. They took a long time to recognise and identify their visual sensations.

Gregory (1963) studied a highly motivated man, S.B., who learned to perceive quickly after regaining his sight. He probably adapted so quickly because he had previously used all his senses in giving meaning to his sensations (cross-modal transfer).

> **Evaluation**
> Again, these studies tell us that adults can learn to perceive. They do not tell us if a new-born child (neonate) inherits or learns perception.

3 Animal studies/deprivation studies

Animal studies go on the idea that if an animal is deprived of sensory stimulus, which is later restored, the animal might learn to perceive. Psychologists could therefore draw conclusions about whether perception is learned or innate, depending on the animal behaviour (but see comment below).

Blakemore and Cooper (1966) reared kittens in the dark, so that they could see only a 'vertical world'. The kittens grew up seeing only vertical objects, but not horizontal ones.

Hubel and Wiesel discovered that if an animal was deprived of visual stimulation, this would prevent normal development of receptive fields on the retina.

Held and Hein invented the 'kitten carousel', in which one kitten was active and another was restricted in movement. The active kitten developed normal perception, while the passive one did not.

Riesen raised chimps in goggles which allowed in enough light to let their eyeballs develop, but did not let them see anything. The chimps did not seem to develop complex perceptual abilities.

36 *Personal Processes*

> **Evaluation**
> None of these studies tells us how perception develops. Animals cannot tell us what they perceive, so we cannot draw general conclusions, nor can we transfer those conclusions to ideas about human perception.

4 Cross cultural studies

Studies indicate that people from different cultures seem to develop different perceptual abilities.

Turnbull (1961) discovered that pygmies seemed not to have size constancy. When they saw a herd of buffalo in the distance, they thought they were ants.

Segal, Campbell and Herskowitz (1973) tested the perception of Europeans and Zulus, using the Müller-Lyer illusion. The Europeans perceived the lines as different lengths; the Zulus perceived them as the same length. This could be because Europeans are brought up in a carpentered environment (see Unit 2), and would expect to see angles and other depth cues which aid perspective, but Zulus would not, because, instead of the angles and straight lines of the manufacturing culture of the Western world, their environment was made up of trees and other features of their natural world.

Hudson (1967) found that many African tribes drew pictures of animals and objects 'flat', rather than 3-dimensional.

> **Evaluation**
> These studies do not indicate that the perception of one culture is better than another, simply that people seem to develop perceptual and other skills depending on their interaction with their own familiar environment.

5 Studies of human infants (neonates)

This is probably the most sensible way to draw conclusions about whether perception in humans is innate or learned.

Gibson and Walk (1960) tested depth perception by placing babies on a device incorporating a 'visual cliff'. Babies refused to crawl over the 'deep' side.

Fantz (1966) showed infants face shapes which had different degrees of human characteristics. He concluded that infants preferred looking at an 'organised' face rather than a jumbled or shaded face shape.

Bower (1966) played peek-a-boo with babies to see if they could recognise and react to cubes. He discovered that even very young babies had some size and shape constancy.

4 Evaluation

These are all very interesting studies, yet we are no closer to understanding whether perception is inherited or learned. Comparative studies with animals and other cultures do not help us to understand, because (a) animals cannot tell us what they are experiencing, and (b) cultures have their own particular ways, and cannot usefully be compared with others.

From all these studies it would appear that nature and nurture interact. Certain perceptual skills, such as size and shape constancy, appear to be innate (but what about Turnbull's work?), whereas others appear to be learned.

What is your experience? Have you ever had to learn to perceive something, or did your perception simply come about naturally? Think of some everyday examples of these issues, and try to relate them to the studies you have read about here.

5 Summary

How do we come to have our perceptual abilities? How does perception develop?

Evidence is offered through

1 **perceptual adaptation or re-adjustment studies:** *Stratton, Köhler, Hess*

2 **human cataract patient studies:** *Von Senden, Gregory*

3 **animal studies/deprivation studies:** *Blakemore and Cooper, Hubel and Wiesel, Held and Hein, Riesen*

4 **cross-cultural studies:** *Turnbull, Segall, Campbell and Herskowitz, Hudson*

5 **studies of human infants:** *Gibson and Walk, Fantz, Bower*

6 Now ⟶ Over to you ....

1 *Fill in the missing words*

Empiricists believe that perception is .... Nativists believe that perception is ....

2 *Choose the correct answer*

Both Stratton and Köhler adapted to the special spectacles probably because
    (a) they liked them.
    (b) they learned to perceive in a new way.
    (c) they saw everything upside down and in different colours.

3 *Choose the correct answer*

The patients of Von Senden and Gregory reacted in different ways when their sight was restored because
    (a) they had regained their sight after cataract operations.
    (b) they were mature.
    (c) they learned to adapt to their new environment.

4 *Complete the sentence*

Animal studies do not help us particularly in saying whether perception is learned or innate because ....
....

5 *Is this statement true or false?*

Cross cultural studies tell us that culture and environment have a significant bearing on how we perceive.

6 *Fill in the missing words*

The studies of G.......................... and W............................ show that babies have depth perception. The studies of F.......................... show that babies like 'organised' faces rather than jumbled patterns. The studies of B............................ show that babies have size and shape constancy.

7 *Is this sentence true or false?*

There is evidence to support the empiricist and the nativist view whether perception is innate or learned, but there is no one definite answer.

7 Written exercises

1 Why do you think Stratton adapted to wearing the inverted goggles?
2 Why do you think Von Senden's patients and Gregory's patients reacted in different ways when their sight was restored?
3 What does the work of Held and Hein tell us about the need for active exploration of the environment by animals?
4 Why do you think the pygmy in Turnbull's study was distressed when he saw the buffalo 'getting bigger'?
5 Give a possible explanation why young babies do not move over the 'deep' side of Gibson and Walk's visual cliff.

8 Topics for discussion

1. What kind of evidence is there in psychology to support the idea that perception is innate or learned?

2. What are your views on the nature-nurture debate in perception?

3. Why must we be cautious in drawing too definite conclusions?

9 Need to know

▷ Can you explain the difference between sensation and perception?

▷ Can you say what the different perspectives are regarding the nature-nurture debate in perception?

▷ Can you name all the psychologists mentioned in this unit and give a description of their work?

10 Suggestions for coursework

1 Carry out an observational study on an infant, replicating Bower's work. See if you can show that the infant actually does perceive shapes. (Remember: to carry out coursework like this, you may need to have direct access to babies or young children, or work with someone who has access to babies or young children. You will need to acknowledge their help on your coursework cover sheet if you work

with someone else; and you must obtain permission to do this kind of study from the child's parent. There are serious ethical issues which must be considered here.)

2 Carry out a survey amongst the class about whether they believe that perception is innate or learned.

More challenging studies

1 Trace the ability of a child to draw over the period of two or three months. Observe how the child develops her/his ability to draw faces, say, or shapes of objects more accurately. Make some suggestions whether the development might have come about as a natural part of maturation, or whether a particular environment might have helped perceptual development. You would be carrying out a case study, using observational techniques to indicate certain behaviours that might or might not change over time.

2 Carry out an investigation into whether perception can be encouraged through experience. You will need to work with two groups of children. Let Group A play with different shaped objects, such as a tetrahedron, a cube, a pyramid. You will need 10-15 of these different shaped objects. Encourage the children to name the objects as they play with them.

Now take a cardboard box with a hole cut in one side, large enough to let a small arm go through. Place the different shaped objects inside the box. Ask children from Group A to feel the objects inside, and name them. They may then draw the object out of the box, and score how many they got right. Ask Group B to do the same. If Group A score higher than Group B, you might suggest that the previous experience of playing with the shapes encouraged a more sensitive perceptual ability to develop. Beware of saying that this is conclusive proof, however!

Unit Four
Learning – Behaviourist approaches

This topic deals with the questions

How do we learn?
Is our behaviour a set of learned responses to specific stimuli?

Learning is generally defined as 'a relatively permanent change in behaviour due to past experience'. We have to add the words 'due to past experience' because you could have a relatively permanent change of behaviour (such as working in a new place, playing more sport because you switched to contact lenses from conventional spectacles) which has nothing to do with experience.

There are two major approaches to learning theory

  behaviourist
  cognitive

This unit examines behaviourist approaches to learning. Unit 5 which follows examines cognitive and other approaches to learning.

The main topics in this unit are

1 the background to behaviourist approaches to learning theory
2 classical conditioning and how it works
3 operant conditioning and how it works
4 reinforcement and how to organise it for maximum effect

1 The background to behaviourist approaches to learning theory

1 Comparative psychology

Comparative psychology compares human behaviour with animal behaviour. This is the foundation for behaviourism in general. Behaviourism is the name given to an approach that believes that studying behaviour is enough to understand psychology; in other words, we understand how people think by observing and noting their behaviour. You need to think about this. Just because people behave in a certain way does not mean that they want to or intend to behave in that way.

Things become even more difficult if we think that we can understand human behaviour by observing animal behaviour. The big questions here are:

Do animals and people behave in the same way?
Can we believe that animals and people learn in the same way?

2 Learning theory

Behaviourists think that

animals and people learn in the same way;
most human behaviour is learned.

Immediate criticisms of this view are that

❐ We cannot know that animals have learned - that is, that they behave in a certain way as a result of learning. They can't tell us what is happening, so we might be mistaken in concluding that they behave as they do as a result of learning.

❐ It may therefore be irresponsible to believe that we can compare animal and human behaviour and say definitely that they behave like that because they learn in the same way.

Behaviourists reply that we don't need to know what animals/people are thinking. The most important thing is that we watch their behaviour, from which we can infer what they are thinking. This narrow view of learning theory is not accepted by many psychologists from the cognitive and social learning approaches.

2 Classical conditioning and how it works

Classical conditioning is the foundation for a theory of learning that associates two events, a particular stimulus with a particular response: therefore it is often called stimulus-response learning. Pavlov, in 1911, was one of the first psychologists to study this systematically.

Basic principles of classical conditioning

1 Reflex stage: an unconditioned* stimulus (neutral, without conditions) leads to an unconditioned response (reflex, without conditions).

* Note Some textbooks use the words 'conditional' and 'unconditional'

neutral stimulus	basic reflex
e.g. food	salivation
unconditioned stimulus	unconditioned response

2 Conditioning phase: a conditioned stimulus is paired with the unconditioned stimulus, leading to an unconditioned response.

conditioned stimulus + neutral stimulus (unconditioned)	basic reflex
e.g. bell + food	salivation

3 Learned phase: the conditioned stimulus will now produce the same response, which has now become a conditioned response.

conditioned stimulus	conditioned response
e.g. bell	salivation

In shorthand terms:

food	salivation
UCS	UCR
bell + food	salivation
CS UCS	UCR
bell	salivation
CS	CR

Quick tip: When you write an exercise or examination answer that asks you to match the letters CS, UCS, CR, UCR with the identified stimulus and response, you must *always* end up with **CS CR** ('Come sun, come rain').

Try this exercise: If I snap my fingers in front of your face, you will automatically blink. Now I want to condition you to blink when I say your name.

What are the **UCS, CS, UCR, CR?**

Reflex stage	UCS (snap of fingers)	UCR (blink)
Conditioning phase	CS (name) + UCS (snap of fingers)	UCR (blink)
Learned phase	CS (name)	CR (blink)

Generalisation

This is the name given to the tendency to generalise the learning to other stimuli. In Pavlov's experiments, he found that the dogs would salivate when they heard any bell. The closer the new bell sound was to the original bell sound, the stronger the salivation response would be. In our example, you might blink in response to the sound of my voice saying anything, as well as your name. The closer whatever I said was to the sound of your name, the stronger your response of blinking would be. This variety in the strength of the response is known as the **generalisation gradient**. The closer the new stimulus is to the original one, the stronger the response.

Discrimination

This is the term given to the ability to tell the difference between two stimuli. Pavlov found that he could train his dogs to discriminate between different shapes, by reinforcing one response and not the other. In our example, you might blink in response when I say your name, but you might not blink to someone else saying your name.

Extinction (unlearning, forgetting)

This happens when we stop pairing the CS + UCS over time. The conditioned response breaks down. When you hear your name you no longer blink. To prevent extinction (forgetting) we have to 'top up' the CS by presenting the UCS as well from time to time. For example, you are used to having a pudding after your evening meal (end of meal = CS; arrival of pudding = CR), that is, until you decide to go on a diet and stop eating pudding. The end of the meal will still make you think that the pudding is next, until you get used to not eating pudding. Your expectation will die out (possibly!) and you will unlearn that particular response. (Don't feel you have to try this out in practice; just learn the theory, and enjoy your pudding.)

One trial learning

This is a particularly quick way of learning something immediately. If you touch the surface of a hot oven, you very quickly learn that the experience is uncomfortable and you immediately learn not to do it again. We learn many things in this way, such as not poking our fingers into empty light sockets, or not teasing the cat. Once bitten, twice shy.

3 Operant conditioning and how it works

Operant conditioning was the name coined by **B.F. Skinner.** He also referred to **instrumental conditioning**. Both terms are interchangeable. Thorndike referred to the **Law of Effect.** The terms *operant conditioning, instrumental conditioning* and *law of effect* refer to the same thing; it is important, however, that you know which term was used by which psychologist.

The main difference between classical conditioning and operant conditioning is that **classical conditioning** involves reflex actions only, whilst **operant conditioning** involves voluntary responses. For example, a learning experience which could be put down to classical conditioning would be if I learned to associate seeing Jack with seeing Jill; they both go around together all the time; or if I learned to associate getting up when the alarm rings. These are not particularly voluntary responses (I might not want to get up when the alarm rings). A learning experience which could be put down to operant conditioning would be this: I associate some reward with doing particularly well in my studies (my parents give me a rise in weekly allowance), so I intentionally work harder in order to do better.

Both Skinner and Thorndike demonstrated that it is possible to train rats, pigeons and other animals to behave in certain ways through reinforcing (rewarding) desired behaviour. But remember the comment in (1) above: can we assume that humans learn in the same way as animals?

Note — Remember - It is very important to appreciate that both classical and operant conditioning have nothing to do with cognitive responses - i.e. thinking things through. Conditioning of any form goes on the idea of stimulus-response.

3 Reinforcement and how to organise it for maximum effect

In classical conditioning, **reinforcement** is the strengthening of the likelihood of a response. Pairing the UCS with the CS is the reinforcement. If we do not continue to pair the UCS + CS from time to time, the CR will become extinct. This is called the **Law of Exercise** - we learn something that is presented many times.

In operant conditioning, reinforcement is the strengthening of the likelihood of a response, and also can be used to **'shape'** behaviour - that is, bring about a desired behaviour in small steps.

Schedules of reinforcement

The idea of **schedules of reinforcement** is about organising reinforcement to produce the desired behaviour.

There are two main types of reinforcement

> **interval,** referring to the timing of reinforcement
> **ratio,** referring to how many times reinforcement happens

The schedules, either interval or ratio, can be **fixed or variable:** that is, occurring for fixed or variable lengths of time, and occurring at fixed and variable intervals.

Whichever schedule is used influences the rate of response ('learning') and also influences how resistant it is to extinction ('remembering').

Schedule	When reinforcer presented	Response rate (How quickly learned)	Extinction resistance
1 continuous	every correct response	fast	low
2 fixed ratio	every so many correct responses	fast	moderate
3 variable ratio	variable number	fast	high
4 fixed interval	every so much time, as long as one correct response is produced.	slow	moderate
5 variable interval	varied amount of time between reinforcements	steady	high

Primary and secondary reinforcement

Primary reinforcement refers to reinforcement which satisfies a basic need or drive, such as hunger, thirst, sex, approval. Primary reinforcements directly affect behaviour.

Secondary reinforcement is the reinforcement of something which is associated with the satisfaction of basic needs, such as money.

Sometimes a secondary reinforcement, such as money, turns into a primary reinforcement - something to be desired in itself: the secondary reinforcement (money) is associated with the primary reinforcement (success) and becomes a basic need.

Negative reinforcement

This is a real danger area, and you should be quite clear about what negative reinforcement refers to. Positive reinforcement rewards appropriate behaviour and encourages it. Negative reinforcement is **the avoidance of an unpleasant stimulus.** It is **not** punishment (see below).

Examples of negative reinforcement

You know your parents will be concerned if you go out before doing your homework, so you always do your homework first. You avoid the consequences of unacceptable behaviour.

You know you will burn your hands if you pick up the dish straight from the oven (you did once!), so you always wear oven gloves.

Escape learning

This is learning from an unpleasant situation. If I am in my neighbour's garden, about to help myself to apples from his tree, and I see him coming out of his house, I will jump over the nearest fence. His appearance is the stimulus I need to make me escape.

Avoidance learning

In fact, his appearance is the stimulus I need to make me avoid going in the garden in the first place. I know what he can be like! The avoidance of his temper is a very powerful reinforcement of the behaviour which enables me to avoid it.

Punishment

There are two views about whether punishment is a reinforcer, and therefore part of learning theory. One view says that punishment has nothing at all to do with learning or reinforcement. It is a behaviour of the punisher - not of the person or animal which is on the receiving end (the learner). Punishment is applied to try to suppress other people's behaviour. In terms of social situations and social psychology, punishment may well be a very important factor. In terms of learning theory, punishment is not a factor.

Another view says that punishment can bring about behaviour change, and therefore can fit our definition of learning and act as a reinforcer. Try to think of examples from your everyday experience to draw your own conclusion about this.

4 Evaluation

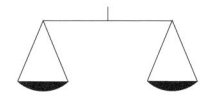

Comparative psychology is taken as the foundation for a lot of psychological enquiry. This is not entirely safe, as we have pointed out, because there is no way that humans can know what animals are experiencing when we say that they 'learn' something. It is also too simple to think that humans learn in the same way that animals do. Therefore comparative psychology might not be the best basis for an understanding of what happens when humans learn - i.e. learning theory in humans.

Behaviourism has been a major influence in psychology for the last fifty years and more. It is very tempting to see behaviour as the evidence of how people are thinking and feeling. This is, however, not necessarily so. Behaviourism has been strongly criticised by many psychologists, often with justification, and sometimes without. It would appear that some human action occurs as a result of very primitive learning mechanisms, such as stimulus-response, but it would be unwise to say that all human action occurs on this basis. Behaviourism is an extreme point of view.

Nevertheless, behaviourism has been put into practice quite effectively in many different forms and therefore should not be dismissed out of hand. For example, token economies, merit systems in schools, and programmed learning all operate on the basic principles of behaviourism.

5 Summary

How do we learn? Is our behaviour a set of responses to specific stimuli?

1 Behaviourist approaches are based on comparative psychology and its implications for learning theory.

2 Classical conditioning (*Pavlov*) involves the principles of

conditioned stimulus, conditioned response, unconditioned stimulus, unconditioned response

the pattern is   UCS   UCR
                      CS + UCS   UCR
                          CS   CR

Generalisation is the name given to when we respond to other stimuli that are similar to the original stimulus.

Discrimination is the name given to the ability to tell the difference between stimuli that are similar, and to respond to one rather than another.

One trial learning is a particular kind of quick and effective learning that can be seen as classical conditioning.

Extinction is the name given to the process of forgetting, when the CS loses its strength so that the CR is not maintained.

3 Operant conditioning (*Skinner, Thorndike*) follows similar principles to classical conditioning, but operates on the basis of voluntary behaviour, and often involves the idea of desired behaviour as an outcome of a desired reward. Behaviour can therefore be induced, predicted and controlled.

4 Reinforcement and how to organise it for maximum effect

Schedules of reinforcement can be organised in terms of fixed or variable intervals or ratios.

The most effective schedules for lasting effect (learning) are variable ratios and intervals. As soon as anything, including rewards, becomes routine, we tend to lose interest and stop trying so hard. It seems that we need to keep up a high level of commitment in order to learn most efficiently, and for the learning curve to be maintained, and this is best achieved if rewards are not taken for granted. Uncertainty can be a great incentive!

5 Other aspects of reinforcement are the difference between primary and secondary reinforcement, and when one might turn into the other. Negative reinforcement is the avoidance of an unpleasant stimulus. Escape learning and avoidance learning are self-explanatory, and both part of the idea of reinforcement.

6 Punishment is not necessarily part of learning theory, although it can bring about behaviour change, and therefore can be seen as a reinforcer.

6   Now ⟶ Over to you ...

1 Fill in the missing words

There are two main approaches to learning theory: the b..................... approach and the c.......................... approach.

2 *Choose the correct answer from the choices*

Comparative psychology is about

(a)   comparing pets' behaviour with their owners' behaviour;
(b)   believing that the study of animal behaviour can be taken as the foundation for the study of human behaviour;
(c)   studying how to train animals most effectively.

3 *Using the terms UCS, UCR, CS, CR, fill in the blanks which describe Pavlov's work with dogs:*

             food   salivation
             ....

      bell + food   salivation
     ....

             bell   salivation
             ....

4 *Complete the following sentences*

(a) Generalisation is the name given ....

(b) Discrimination is what happens when we ....

(c) Extinction happens when we..

(d) An example of one trial learning is when...

5 *Which of these statements are true and which are false?*

(a) Continuous reinforcement is very effective for bringing about sustained learning.
(b) Fixed interval reinforcement has a slow response rate.
(c) Variable interval reinforcement is very efficient in bringing about learning.
(d) The most effective reinforcement schedules are variable ratio and variable reinforcement.

6 *Fill in the missing words*

A **s**........................ reinforcer can become a **p**................ reinforcer when it becomes something to be desired in itself. An example of this is m . . . y.

7 *Complete the sentence*

Negative reinforcement is the ....
....

7 Written exercises

1 Apply the labels UCS, CS, UCR, CR to the following situations:
   (a) Every morning for a week you receive a letter from your latest girl/boyfriend through the post. You are very happy. By Friday your heart jumps even when you hear the postman open the gate.
   (b) You are anxious about taking an important examination. Sometimes you get butterflies in the tummy even when you pass by the room where it will be held.
2 What are the similarities and differences between classical and operant conditioning? Give examples in your answer.
3 With reference to schedules of reinforcement, can you say why gambling might become addictive?
4 Give three examples of secondary reinforcers, and say how they might become primary reinforcers.

8 Topics for discussion

1 Do you think comparative psychology (comparing animals and humans) is relevant to learning theory?

2 Do you think the idea of stimulus response learning may be generally applied to humans? Give some examples of instances when it might be so.

3 What value do you see for punishment? Is punishment necessary?

9 Need to know

➮ Can you say why comparative psychology might or might not be the best basis for an understanding of the way that humans learn?

➮ Can you identify some of the strengths and weaknesses of behaviourism as a way of thinking in psychology?

☞ Can you explain clearly the difference between classical and operant conditioning? What other names are there for operant conditioning? Which psychologists do we associate with these terms?

☞ Could you analyse any classical conditioning situation in terms of UCS, UCR, CS, CR?

☞ Can you identify the various schedules of reinforcement, and say which ones are most efficient in terms of learning?

☞ Can you explain what negative reinforcement is?

10 Suggestions for coursework

Note: In undertaking coursework on this topic, you must be very careful to follow the ethical guidelines laid down by the various Psychological Associations. You must not experiment on or with animals. You may observe without interfering, but you must not manipulate the behaviour of animals in any way.

1 Conduct a simple learning task where certain responses are positively reinforced and others aren't. Then test to see if the reinforced responses are recalled better than the others.

2 Conduct an investigation to test the hypothesis, 'Positive reinforcement will improve the number skills of college students (or another group)'.

3 Conduct an observational study to test the hypothesis, 'Students will respond more frequently in class if they are positively reinforced'. Remember to identify the different categories of behaviour you are observing, and draw up an observation schedule so that you can tally the number of responses that you observe.

More challenging studies

1 Carry out an observational study of people undertaking a learning task. This could be watching children playing sport (remember to get the usual permissions from the parents or Headteacher where necessary), and see how many times the instructor rewards their performance with 'Good' or 'Well done.' Say what kind of effect this might have on the children. Or trace your own performance as a learner and say how you react to reward. Or watch youngsters, or even animals, learning how to, say, climb trees, or catch a ball, and how their desired behaviour spurs them on to greater effort. Or watch adults with children in a public place, and observe whether the adults engage in rewarding behaviour. An interesting twist here is to see when children sometimes get their own way in response to 'I

want ... !' and thus reward adults for buying them the desired object by being good.

2 Carry out an investigation into how desired behaviour is encouraged in a school, an office or an institution. Get permission from the managers to examine the rewards system (gold stars, mention in weekly log, promotion options, etc.) and say whether the rewards system actually does encourage desired behaviour outcomes. You might then extend this study by conducting a survey or questionnaire involving the children, or employees, to see whether they feel that the rewards system already in place encourages appropriate behaviour, or whether the rewards system could be reviewed and improved. Remember that this kind of investigation has to be conducted with great sensitivity to people's feelings, but it can be most interesting, particularly if undertaken in collaboration with the managers of the institution.

3 Conduct a survey to find out if people buy a particular product as a result of seeing or hearing the product advertised. Draw some conclusions from your findings as to whether you feel people are conditioned to buy a product through advertising. Can consumerism be related to conditioning? Do we learn to pay attention to advertising? For that matter, do we learn to be conditioned?

Unit Five
Learning – Cognitive and ethological approaches

This unit deals with the questions

How do we learn?
Is our behaviour the result of cognition (thinking) and/or innate capacities?

Behavioural approaches to learning (Unit 4) suggest that learning happens as the result of matching particular responses with specific stimuli. Cognitive approaches offer different explanations to S-R theories. The main ideas are

1. Humans have some kind of innate mental mapping process (***Tolman***);
2. Humans learn to imitate by watching other people (***Bandura***);
3. Humans learn because of sudden insights (***Köhler***);
4. Humans learn because they are ready to (***Harlow***).

These theories still use the idea of comparative psychology, as behaviourist approaches do, saying that it is possible to transfer ideas about animal behaviour to humans.

The main themes in this topic are

1. Can cognitive approaches to learning theory help us to understand and explain human behaviour?
2. Can ethological approaches to learning theory help us to understand and explain human behaviour?

1 Cognitive approaches to learning theory

1 Latent Learning Theory

Tolman (1932) allowed rats to become familiar with a maze, without any reinforcement of any particular behaviour. When he placed food in the maze the rats found their way around the maze more quickly than rats who had the same experience of the maze but without a food reward. He suggested that the rats had 'internalised' a 'map', and said that learning had taken place without reinforcement - a challenge to S-R theories. The rats had learned the information but kept it latent until they needed it.

2 Observational Learning Theory (see also Social Learning Theory)

Bandura (1973) suggested that children learned to imitate adults through observational learning. This is called **modelling.** Like Tolman, he thought that no reinforcement was necessary for learning to take place.

Bandura's work has serious implications for current debates on how people's behaviour (especially children's) might be influenced by TV violence, family arguments, whether models like Batman are socially acceptable, if comics with characters like Judge Dredd are damaging, and so on.

3 Insight Learning

Köhler (1925) investigated **insight learning** in chimpanzees. He showed that the animals were able to use sticks and other instruments to reach fruit. This behaviour appeared to be organised, and Köhler suggested that the chimps had 'worked out' how to solve the problem of reaching the fruit - that is, they showed insight. Often they seemed to ponder, come to a sudden realisation and then act - what Köhler called an 'Aha!' experience.

4 Learning sets

Harlow (1949), also working with monkeys, investigated how **learning sets** might develop. He trained monkeys to solve 'odd-one-out' problems, and found that they soon seemed to learn a general strategy how to do this. He suggested that they were **learning how to learn** - that is, developing a learning set. 'Learning how to learn' is a cognitive activity, and has nothing to do with S-R.

2 Ethological approaches to learning theory

Ethology refers to the study of behaviour in the natural environment, both for human and non-human animals. The ethological approach suggests that some behaviours are innate. In animals, these are known as **fixed action patterns** (FAPs).

Fixed action patterns

Tinbergen (1951), for example, studied animals, including fish and birds, and showed that some behaviours are triggered by certain sign stimuli - e.g. a red spot on a fish's belly acted as the stimulus to trigger an attack by another fish; young chicks in certain bird species peck at a parent's beak to make the parent regurgitate food. There are a number of wildlife documentaries on TV these days that show this kind of behaviour. Desmond Morris, for example, claims that a whole range of human behaviour also follows such fixed action patterns, though this is by no means sure.

Other evidence for ethological theories of learning is:

Imprinting - *Lorenz* (1930) demonstrated that animals would attach themselves to the first moving object they saw. Imprinting took place during a specific critical period.

Aggression - certain aggressive behaviours appear to be common among animals (and among humans?). *Lorenz* felt that aggression was natural in animals and humans, and many psychologists agree. **Calhoun** (1962), for example, investigated the idea of the **aggression-frustration hypothesis,** when rats became more aggressive as they were deprived of space. Calhoun transferred this idea to humans. It could be relevant to issues such as inner-city violence.

Territoriality - many animals mark out their own territory and vigorously defend it against invasion by other animals.

3 Evaluation

It is tempting to think that we can understand human behaviour as a direct parallel of animal behaviour. There really is no foundation for this.

Cognitive theories of learning, drawn from animal studies, suggest that animals can think. This raises several questions, including what we mean by 'thinking'. While there is no evidence that animals do act rationally, there is also no evidence that they do not. What we choose to believe as psychologists depends on the conclusions we draw from our observations, but it is not a good idea to put forward those conclusions as proof. All we can do is offer ideas as to how things might be, rather than definite answers as to how things are.

Ethological approaches to learning theory can also be quite extreme in their conclusions. It is easy to suppose that humans have fixed action patterns, as some animals have, but perhaps this is just an easy option and needs to be regarded with some caution. Human action is usually part of a situation or context, so to say that humans act only out of instinct, as some animals might do, is too simple.

4 Summary

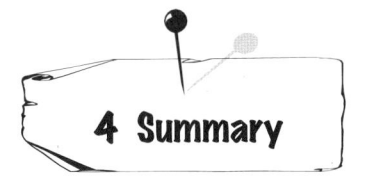

How do we learn?
Is our behaviour the result of cognition (thinking) and/or innate capacities?

Challenges to behavioural approaches are these:

1 Can cognitive approaches to learning theory help us to understand and explain human behaviour?

✧ *Tolman's* latent learning theory says that animals can develop cognitive maps. This learning has nothing to do with stimulus-response.
✧ *Bandura's* social learning theory says that behaviour is learned by imitation.
✧ *Köhler* suggests that animals (and humans by implication) reason things out.
✧ *Harlow* suggests that animals (and humans by implication) develop strategies for learning how to learn.

2 Can ethological approaches to learning theory help us to understand and explain human behaviour?

✧ *Tinbergen* and *Lorenz*, among others, say that animals behave out of instinct. Characteristics such as identification with care-givers (imprinting in animals; bonding in humans), aggression and territoriality are in-built. They suggest that this idea may be transferred to humans.

5 Now ⇒ Over to you ...

1 *Match the statement with the psychologist*

(a)	Humans have some kind of innate mental mapping process	(i)	Bandura
(b)	Humans learn to imitate by watching other people	(ii)	Köhler
(c)	Humans learn because of sudden insights	(iii)	Harlow
(d)	Humans learn because they are ready to	(iv)	Tolman

2 *Fill in the missing words in this passage*

Ethology refers to the study of human and non-human animal b............ in the natural e..................., and suggests that some behaviours are i............... In animals these are known as F............. A.............

P............................ Some psychologists who have investigated this idea are T...................., who observed the behaviour of sticklebacks; L........................, who studied imprinting, and C....................., who studied the behaviour of rats. He investigated the idea of the a......................-f......................... hypothesis, which is when rats became more aggressive when they were deprived of space.

3 Fill in the missing words, and then complete the sentence

Both c................................. and e.......................... approaches to learning theory challenge the idea of behaviourism, because.............
....
....

4 Only one of the following answers is untrue. Which one?

(a) Behaviourism is the name given to the study of human behaviour.
(b) Cognitive approaches to learning theory say that behaviour is related to thinking.
(c) Ethological approaches to learning theory believe that some human behaviour, like some animal behaviour, is due to Fixed Action Patterns.
(d) Stimulus-response approaches to learning theory say that some responses are innate.

5 Unscramble the names of these psychologists

Zlorne, Warhol, Noulhac, Abnadur, Moltan

6 Written exercises

1 Tolman is called both a behaviourist and a cognitive psychologist. Can you say why?
2 What might be an implication of Bandura's observational learning theory for the education of children?
3 Köhler claimed that the chimps were 'thinking about' the problem, and then reached a conclusion. Others maintain that the chimps responded to a collection of stimuli. Others say that they found a solution simply by trial and error. What do you think and why?
4 Harlow claimed that the monkeys were building up learning strategies. He has been challenged on this. Is it possible that the monkeys were developing a general learning ability, or were they responding to generalised patterns of stimuli?
5 Name any three fixed action patterns that you have observed in animals. Have you observed any FAPs in humans?

7 Topics for discussion

1. Is it possible for animals to think - that is, undertake cognitive activity, or is everything they do a response to stimuli, to a greater or lesser degree?

2. Is it ever possible to judge that learning has taken place simply by observing behaviour?

3. All learning theory mentioned in this unit (except observational learning theory) is based on comparative psychology. This raises the question of whether it is possible to transfer theories of animal learning to theories of human learning. Do you think this is reasonable, or is there room for doubt?

4. Some psychologists say that we can understand the way humans learn by watching the way that animals learn. What arguments could you offer for or against this view?

5. The nature-nurture debate continues about whether learning happens as a result of innate processes, cognitive processes (innate or acquired), or responses to specific stimuli. What do you think?

8 Need to know

➪ Can you explain how cognitive approaches differ from behaviourist approaches?

➪ Can you explain how ethological approaches differ from both behaviourist and cognitive approaches?

➪ Can you name all the psychologists mentioned in this unit, and give an accurate description of their work?

➪ Can you give a critical evaluation of the strengths and weaknesses of (a) comparative psychology and (b) ethological approaches as a foundation for the study of human mind and behaviour?

9 Suggestions for coursework

1 Conduct an observational study of any situation in which children and adults are together. Tally the number of instances the children imitate the behaviour of the adults. You can do this by watching a real-life situation, or by watching television. Remember to use categories of behaviour.

2 Conduct another observational study of any situation in which adults imitate the behaviour of other adults. Talk about the idea of social learning theory as a possible basis for this kind of behaviour.

3 Construct a maze learning task using two pieces of card, one with a maze drawn on it and the other with a small hole in it -

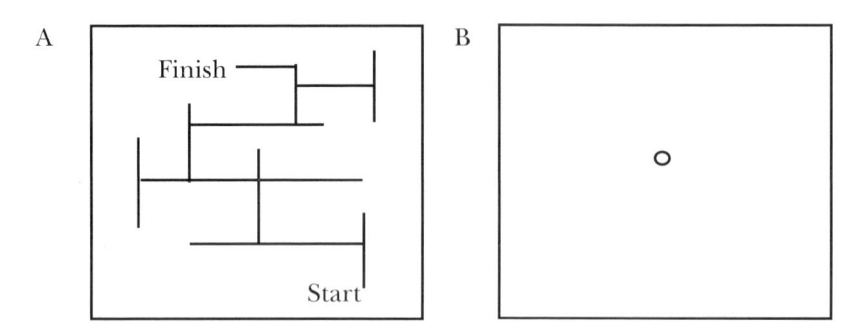

Place card B over card A so that participants cannot see the whole maze. They have to move card B around so that they can find their way through the maze by looking through the hole. Divide participants into two groups and have each group learn the maze by trial and error. After, say, 10 attempts, tell one group that they will be rewarded for navigating the maze correctly. Compare the performance of both groups.

More challenging studies

1 Conduct a survey, gathering attitudes of people to programmes on television which show violence. Find out whether people feel these programmes ought to be censored or monitored in some way. You could investigate people's attitudes to cartoons, or comics, or Disney and other animated films. You could ask people if they feel that a greater number of socially acceptable role models ought to be presented through the media. You might find it helpful to draw up an attitude scale as part of the data gathering.

2 Carry out an investigation/experiment into the way that children/adults learn by inviting a group of children and a group of adults to solve puzzles. These puzzles could be visual-spatial, or condundrums, or manipulative ones such as the Rubik Cube. Compare the performance of both groups.

Unit Six
Memory – What is it and how does it work?

This unit deals with the questions

What is memory? How does it work?

Most of us tend to think of memory as an object and something to do with the past. This is not so. Memory is definitely something that is going on in the present - it is an active process.

One of the difficulties in studying memory is the use of words. The word 'memory' has at least three different uses. It is used to refer to the processing and storage of information for later recall; for example, when I say, 'I must remember this date.' It is used to refer to the storage system in which information is held; for example, when I say, 'I have a good memory for dates.' It is also used to refer to the stored information itself; for example, when I say, 'My memory of that date is that it was a sunny day.'

The main themes of this unit are

1. What processes are involved in remembering?
2. What theories help us to understand the process of remembering?
3. How can we improve our memory (our ability to remember)?

1 Processes involved in remembering

Psychologists generally agree that there are three processes involved in remembering:

> **encoding**, by which sensory information is put into the memory;
> **storage,** where the information is held in the memory;
> **retrieval**, when we take the information out of the memory ready for use.

Your computer memory works on these three principles: you input information (it is encoded); you store it; and you retrieve it when it is needed.

Where psychologists disagree is how we actually do remember information. Here are some points of disagreement:

> (a) What are the factors that influence encoding?
> (b) How does the memory function?
> (c) What happens when we wish to retrieve the information?

Let's now look at factors involved in encoding, storing and retrieving.

2 Encoding

Information comes to us via our senses. We have to translate it in some way in order to put it into the memory store.

Bruner (1956) suggested three ways of encoding information:

> **enactive representation** - in this mode we remember experiences in which we have been active;
> **iconic representation** - this is to do with images, the visual experiences we have;
> **symbolic representation** - this is information presented in a more abstract sense, in language and other symbols.

Examples of these modes are:

> ❏ in the enactive mode, I remember how to swim (I remember the physical feelings);
> ❏ in the iconic mode, I remember a picture of my family (I have a mental image);
> ❏ in the symbolic mode, I remember a piece of music (I can experience the feelings it conveys).

A lot of work has been carried out on encoding information, particularly in the area of Bruner's iconic representation - that is, how we can improve memory through visualisation.

Improving memory through imagery (mnemonic systems)

There are a number of different systems to help us to store information using visual images. The most common are these.

> **1 method of loci** - we imagine we are in familiar territory, and place items to be remembered in strategic places within the scene;

2 key word method *(Raugh and Atkinson,* 1975) - we link the sound of a word with the visual image it conjures up;

3 peg word method - a 2-step process involving (i) memorising a set of words that rhyme with the numbers 1-10; these are the pegs to hang other words on; (ii) combining the peg word with the new material to be learned.

Other mnemonic systems can also improve memory, such as rhymes (thirty days hath September ...), or making up a set of words from the first letters of words to be remembered: e.g. Every Good Boy Deserves Favour (the musical scale EGBDF).

> **Useful tip**
>
> In your studies of psychology or other subjects, using mnemonic systems can be a real short-cut to memorising facts and figures. For every item of information you want to remember (store for later retrieval), think up a picture or story around that item. Make the picture or story as meaningful as possible to yourself. Some people find that creating a really silly image helps them to remember the story or image, and the item to be remembered.

Bartlett showed that encoding is an active process; in retelling *'The War of the Ghosts'* people re-created the story for themselves. They were told a story, which they then had to pass on to another person. (This is how the party game *'Chinese Whispers'* works.) As each person took over the story, they kept the pieces of the story that were personally meaningful to them, and cut out the bits that did not make sense. Bartlett suggests that this is what most of us do when we remember information. We commit to memory those bits that are personally meaningful, and also recreate the memory when we retrieve it from storage.

Now let's take a look at storage.

3 Storage

Theories of remembering

There are two main approaches to how storage works:

1. the multi-store model
2. the levels of processing model

1 The multi-store model

Ebbinghaus in the last century was one of the first psychologists to suggest that there are two memory stores - **short term memory (STM)** and **long term memory (LTM).**

Atkinson and Shiffrin (1968) developed a **multi-store model**, saying that information first goes into the STM for temporary use, and can be rehearsed and transferred to the LTM for more permanent storage. Memory was a structure, something like a storage box consisting of several parts, into which information was passed, regardless of its content or whether it was meaningful to the person.

2 The levels of processing model

Craik and Lockhart (1972) suggested that how well we store information depends on how thoroughly we process it when we first receive it (encode it). The more we pay attention to the information, and the more we have to work to make sense of it, the more we are likely to remember it.

This view is supported by the theories of

Bartlett (mentioned above) who demonstrated that remembering is something that people actively do *('The War of the Ghosts')*;

Tulving and Pearlstone who demonstrated that we tend to organise our remembering (they showed how important category headings are in organising information);

Loftus and Loftus who showed that we tend to construct our memories (they asked people to comment on how they remembered a film that they had seen previously);

Carmichael et al. who showed that we remember in terms of the language we use to describe what we perceive (they asked people to describe ambiguous pictures; the people remembered the pictures in terms of the language they had first used).

4 Retrieval

Ebbinghaus (1885) suggested several ways of remembering, that is, retrieving information that has previously been encoded and stored. They were:

> **free recall** - we call up the information from the memory in any order we choose;
> **cued recall** - we associate an item to be remembered with a cue;
> **recognition** - we recognise the item to be remembered out of all the information which is presented to us (an exteme form of cued recall);
> **relearning and savings method** - relearning material takes less time than the original learning of the material did;
> **overlearning** - continuing to learn already learned material results in remembering it more effectively.

Retrieval overlaps into theories of forgetting, which is the focus of the next unit.

5 Evaluation

The biggest problem for most people in studying memory is that they tend to think of it as an object that can be found somewhere in the mind/brain, and this object contains the past, like a box contains souvenirs. This is not the case. Memory is an active process, and what is remembered (retrieved) depends on what is happening to the person who is remembering (retrieving) information.

Theories of memory fall into the two approaches of the multi-store model and the levels of processing model. Criticisms of the multi-store model are that it tends to reinforce the idea of memory as a black box: there are 'compartments' in the 'box' where information is stored. Saying things over and over to yourself doesn't guarantee that they will be remembered later on. The levels of processing model takes into account the human elements of how well the information is learned in the first place. Psychologists like Bartlett have done a lot to show that remembering is a creative exercise, and what is 'remembered' (created) is influenced by the person's mental, emotional and environmental state whilst remembering.

6 Summary

What is memory? How does memory work?

Psychologists tend to agree that there are three processes involved in memory/remembering. These are encoding, storage and retrieval. Psychologists also tend to agree that there are two kinds of memory: short term memory (STM) and long term memory (LTM).

1 Encoding

Bruner suggests that there are 3 ways of encoding

enactive	We remember the body movements involved.

iconic	We have an image of what we are thinking. A lot of work has been done by psychologists to investigate mnenomic systems that help us remember more efficiently:
	    method of loci
	    key word system (***Raugh and Atkinson***)
	    peg word system
	    anagrams

symbolic	We can put our thinking into words

2 Storage

Two main models:

multi-store model (*Atkinson and Shiffrin*)

>   information → STM → LTM

levels of processing model (*Craik and Lockhart*)

see also **Bartlett** (*War of the Ghosts*)
>   **Tulving and Pearlstone** (category headings)
>   **Loftus and Loftus** (constructed memory)
>   **Carmichael et al.** (retrieval can depend on language use in encoding)

3 Retrieval

Ebbinghaus suggests ways of remembering:
>   free recall
>   cued recall
>   recognition
>   relearning savings
>   overlearning

Theories of forgetting (coming in next Unit)

7 Now ━━━▶ Over to You . . .

1 *Fill in the missing words*

Memory is generally believed to consist of three processes: e........................, s.................... and r..........................., and there are two kinds of memory: s...................... t..................... m............... and l............ t................. m........................

2 *Put these three ways of encoding information in the order that Bruner thought they were acquired*

>   iconic representation; enactive representation; symbolic representation

3 *Complete the sentences*

(a) The method of loci works like this: ....
....
....

(b) The key word method works like this: ....
....
(c) The peg word method works like this: ....
....

4 *Match the two theories of remembering with the descriptions given*

(a) the multi-store model (i) this model stresses the importance of actively committing the information to memory
(b) the levels of processing model (ii) this model sees memory as a kind of 'black box' with several compartments

5 *Which of these statements are true and which are false?*

(a) Atkinson and Shiffrin invented the multi-store model.
(b) Craik and Lockhart invented the levels of processing model.
(c) There is not a great deal of difference between the two.
(d) Bartlett showed that ghosts help us to remember.
(e) Tulving and Pearlstone showed the importance of organisation in memory.
(f) Loftus and Loftus asked people to comment on how they remembered a film they had seen previously.
(g) Carmichael *et al.* got people to talk a lot to each other.

8 Written exercises

1 Why is memory described as an active process? Support your answers with reference to specific psychologists.
2 What are Bruner's 3 modes of representation called? Give everyday examples relating to each one.
3 Which mnemonic systems can help us to improve our memory?
4 What are the main differences between the multi-store model and the levels of processing model?
5 Descibe STM and LTM.
6 Describe the ways of remembering that Ebbinghaus suggested.

9 Need to know

▭▷ Can you explain what the three main aspects of memory are?

▭▷ Can you explain the difference between STM and LTM, and say when each is used?

▭▷ Can you describe the difference between the multi-store model and the levels of processing model, and give a critical evaluation of each one?

68 *Personal Processes*

✏ Can you name all the psychologists mentioned in this unit, and describe their work?

✏ Are you sure how the various mnemonic systems mentioned here work, and can you give examples of their use?

10 Topics for discussion

{1} If you wanted to write a book on 'How to improve your memory', what kinds of strategies could you suggest?

{2} What evidence can you offer from your study of psychology that memory is something that we do rather than something that we have?

{3} Do you ever find that you distort your memories as you relive your experiences? Why do you think this is so?

{4} Discuss how anyone might use mnemonic systems for more efficient remembering in courses of study or in everyday life.

11 Suggestions for coursework

1 Try to replicate the 'levels of processing' experiment of Craik and Lockhart.

2 Carry out an investigation like that of Tulving and Pearlstone to see whether category headings really do make a difference in remembering. Give two groups lists of words to learn from an OHP (unrelated samples design). Let one group see the lists of words displayed randomly. For the other group, put the words into categories. Test both groups and record their scores. Draw conclusions about the usefulness of Tulving and Pearlstone's work on the use of category headings in remembering. What implications might studies like this have for real life exercises?

More challenging studies

1 Carry out an investigation like Bartlett's to see if people do re-create a story as they re-tell it. You can do this during a class period. Perhaps ask each member of the group to tell the story into a tape recorder, so that you will have a record of how the story changes.

2 Carry out an experiment to test the effectiveness of the method of loci or the peg word system. Give two separate groups a simple learning task (unrelated samples design), such as remembering lists of words, or dates. For one group, explain how the key word or peg word systems work, and invite them to use the systems in committing the exercise to memory. Test them and keep a record of their scores. Do not tell the other group to use any kind of system. Test them and keep a record of their scores. See if there is a difference in the scores of the two groups, and draw conclusions about whether mnemonic systems do aid memory.

Unit Seven
Remembering and forgetting

This unit deals with the question

Why do we remember some things, and why do we forget some things?

Forgetting occurs when material stored in the memory is not retrieved. Why can we not retrieve it when we want it? Are there some things that we would rather not remember?

Certain factors appear to prevent retrieval, and they are the main topics for this unit:

1 What are the factors affecting retrieval?
2 What theories help us to understand why we forget?

1 Factors affecting retrieval

These seem to be the factors that influence whether or not we remember things.

1 State dependent learning

If we learn something when we are in a particular physiological state (e.g. alert, unwell), we are more likely to remember it when we are in the same state. **Overton** (1972) showed how people who had been under the influence of drink when they committed something to memory could retrieve the information best when they were in the same state again. (We don't recommend this to you as a general learning strategy!) This seems to apply to emotional states as well (e.g. happy, depressed). This is also tied in with -

2 Context dependent learning

If we learn something in a specific context, we are more likely to remember it if we re-create that context. For example, if I learn something while I am at the station waiting for the train, I will be more likely to remember it the next time I am at the station than if I am in the supermarket. This could be because the context provides us with cues. Emotional state is also significant here.

3 Cues and mnemonics

Using mnemonics such as cues helps us to encode the material for storage, and so retrieval of the material is easier. Go back to Unit 6 and check the work of *Raugh and Atkinson*, and *Carmichael et al.*

4 Organisation

Organising the material makes retrieval easier. *Tulving and Pearlstone* (1966) showed the use of cues and organisation in memorising lists of words (see Unit 6).

5 Serial position effect

Items presented in lists will be remembered depending on where they are in the list. The first and last items tend to be remembered better than items appearing in the middle of a list.

2 Theories of forgetting

Psychologists suggest that the main reasons we forget are

1 Decay: the engram (memory trace) fades over time.

2 Brain damage or disease: leading to amnesia. Retrograde amnesia is loss of memory before an event; anterograde amnesia is loss of memory after an event.

    retrograde ⬅ event ➡ anterograde

3 Motivated forgetting: *Freud's* theory (1901) suggests that all forgetting results from repression. The unconscious mind represses unpleasant material so that it seems to be 'forgotten'.

4 Interference: new incoming material interferes with the material already in the memory.

Proactive inteference is when item A (already learned) interferes with item B (to be learned).

Retroactive interference is when item B (just learned) interferes with item A (already learned)

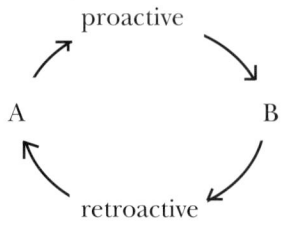

```
           proactive
         ↗         ↘
    A                 B
         ↖         ↙
          retroactive
```

5 Inadequate coding: if the material was not adequately encoded (i.e. if there was no active involvement while committing it to memory) it will not be remembered very efficiently. The work of **Craik and Lockhart** is particularly relevant here (levels of processing), suggesting that how well we retrieve depends on how well we committed the information to memory in the first place.

3 Evaluation

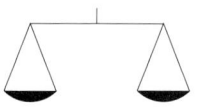

Forgetting is the other side of the coin to remembering. Everything in Unit 6 is relevant here.

Interestingly, **Freud,** out of all the psychologists mentioned, is the only one to suggest that forgetting is an active, deliberate process. Everyone else suggests that forgetting is part of remembering: one of the factors of remembering - encoding - is not carried out as efficiently as it might be. Forgetting is seen as a weakness within the memory system. Freud suggests that forgetting is a healthy activity that protects the mind/brain from overload. This idea may be compared with that of **Crick and Mitchison** (Unit 13), who say that the function of dreaming is to clear the mind/brain of unwanted material that would otherwise clutter it up.

Forgetting may therefore be seen as a passive or active process. What do you think?

Everyone, including Freud, would agree that there is much more in our memories than we can ever recall. Forgetting could result from problems with encoding, storage or retrieval.

Unit Seven Remembering and forgetting 73

4 Summary

Why do we remember some things, and why do we forget some things?

Forgetting seems to be caused by two sets of factors: factors affecting retrieval and reasons for forgetting.

1 Factors affecting retrieval

1 state dependent learning
2 context dependent learning (and emotional state)
3 cues and mnemonics
4 organisation
5 serial position effect

2 Reasons for forgetting (theories of forgetting)

1 decay
2 brain damage or disease (leading to amnesia)
3 motivated forgetting (**Freud**)
4 interference
5 inadequate encoding

5 Now ➔ Over to you...

1 *From the following list, choose five factors which affect whether or not we remember things*

conditioned reflex, state dependent learning, insight learning, perception, context dependent learning, behaviourism, cues and mnemonics, the multi-store model, ethnography, organisation, Fixed Action Patterns, trial and error, serial position effect, aggression-frustration hypothesis, law of effect

2 *Fill in the missing words*

The main reasons we forget are: d.............., br............ da........... or dis..............., mot................ forg...................., in........................, inade................ enc....................

3 *Complete this sentence*

Freud believed that we forget because ....
....

4 *Match the two halves of the jumbled sentences*

Forgetting can result from	retrieval
Freud thought that forgetting was due to	levels of processing
Tulving and Pearlstone showed the effects of	motivation
Cues and mnemonics help	inadequate encoding
Craik and Lockhart said that retrieval depended upon	organisation in memory

6 Written exercises

1 When studying for an examination, how would you take these factors into consideration?
   (a) state dependent learning;
   (b) context dependent learning;
   (c) the importance of cues and mnemonics;
   (d) the importance of organising the material;
   (e) serial position effect.

2 Describe each of the following:
   (a) decay in memory
   (b) amnesia
   (c) motivated forgetting
   (d) interference
   (e) successful encoding for later retrieval

3 Write a letter to a friend, offering good advice for drawing up a revision plan, drawing on your knowledge of theories of remembering and forgetting.

4 How do you think 'memory men and women' manage to perform extraordinary feats of remembering? What strategies do you think they use?

7 Topics for discussion

1. Do you ever deliberately forget things? Why do you do this? Do you think psychologists should pay more attention to the idea that forgetting might be necessary for a healthy mind/brain?

2. How do you think students can be encouraged to remember information? What strategies might they try to help them not to forget?

3. If you wanted to teach someone something, how would you try to make sure that they did not forget it?

8 Need to know

- Can you say what factors are involved in forgetting, and the possible reasons why people forget?
- Can you give a critical evaluation of the theories of why people forget?
- Can you name all the psychologists mentioned in this unit, and describe their work?
- Can you offer some everyday examples of situations when we are more likely to forget than others, and relate these to what you are studying?
- Can you offer commonsense advice, based on what you are studying, to people about how they might not forget information?

9 Suggestions for coursework

1 Carry out an experiment on how interference does interfere with the remembering process. Give two groups of participants a simple learning task. Test one group after the learning task, and keep a record of their scores. Introduce some kind of interference with the other group - perhaps tell them a short story after the learning task, or ask them to do another learning exercise, quite different from the first, before testing them on the first learning exercise. Keep a record of their scores. You might expect the interference to produce lower scores for Group B than for Group A. Which group remembered more?

2 Carry out an experiment on availability vs. accessibility of information in memory. Give one group of participants 25 words to learn. Test their memory by a 'free recall' method. Then mix the original 25 words with another 25 different words and ask them to recognise the original 25 words (repeated measures design). Did they remember more?

3 Carry out an experiment to test the hypothesis, 'Category headings help us to remember lists of items.'

More challenging studies

1 Carry out a survey into the kinds of things that people remember, and the kinds of things they forget. Ask them possible reasons why they forget. You can elaborate on the basic survey by carrying out an attitude test as to whether their emotional reactions to certain items might be a factor in their remembering or forgetting.

2 Carry out an experiment on whether mnemonic systems help us to remember information more successfully. Organise two groups, Group A and Group B. Construct a short advice sheet on how to remember efficiently, using mnemonic techniques. Give this individually to Group A to read. A week later test Group A individually on a memory exercise. Test Group B on the same memory exercise. Then give the information sheet to Group B. As an extension of this study, conduct a survey of both groups, asking if the information sheet was (or might have been) useful in helping them to remember.

Unit Eight
Emotion – physiological foundations

This unit deals with the questions

How do we understand the workings of our brain?
How do the workings of the brain affect the workings of our minds?
Are the two separable?

In psychology, it seems sensible to believe that the body and mind are inseparable. Not everyone believes this. For example, Descartes (pronounced 'Daycart') in the seventeenth century said that the body and mind worked independently, and many people still think they do. However, there is little doubt that our physical state has an influence on our emotions, and our emotional state can have important effects on our physiology. To understand how we experience emotion, and how emotion sometimes turns into stress (see next unit), we first have to understand the physiological foundations for the emotions.

The main themes in this topic are

1 the nervous system
2 structure of the brain
3 studying the brain

1 The nervous system

The nervous system is divided into two main branches, a central and a peripheral system. The peripheral system self-divides into two networks.

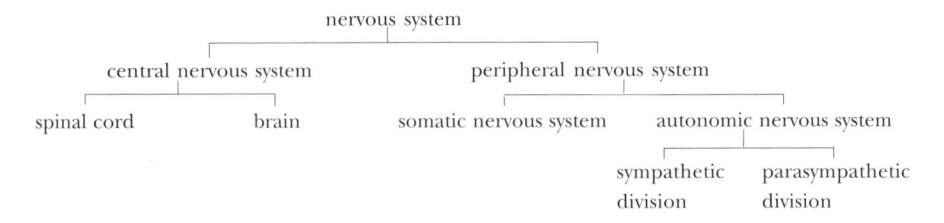

```
                          nervous system
         ┌───────────────────┴───────────────────┐
  central nervous system              peripheral nervous system
    ┌────┴────┐                    ┌──────────────┴──────────────┐
spinal cord  brain        somatic nervous system      autonomic nervous system
                                                       ┌──────────┴──────────┐
                                                   sympathetic        parasympathetic
                                                    division              division
```

The central nervous system (CNS) consists of the brain and spinal cord.
The peripheral nervous system is the system of nerves outside the CNS and consists of

(a) **the somatic nervous system** - a nerve network carrying information to the CNS from the sense organs, and passing information from the brain to the muscles;

(b) **the autonomic nervous system** carrying information from the lower brain to internal glands and organs. It is particularly involved in emotions such as fear, leading to states such as stress.

This is further sub-divided into

- **the sympathetic division** - speeds reactions up;
- **the parasympathetic division** - slows reactions down.

Nerve cells and how they work

The nervous system is made up of millions of **nerve cells** (also called **neurones**). There are three kinds of neurones:

(1) **connector neurones** - carry information from one cell to another;
(2) **sensory neurones** - carry information from sense organs of the body to the brain and spinal cord;
(3) **motor neurones** - carry information from the brain and spinal cord to the muscles of the body, affecting movement.

All neurones pass messages to each other by **synaptic transmission** - i.e. the 'arms' of neurones connect with each other at **synapses,** which are fluid-filled gaps between neurones, sensitive to chemical changes. Chemicals called **neurotransmitters** are released into this gap.

Neurotransmitters serve different functions within the nervous system. There are many different neurotransmitters. The one you particularly need to know for this course is **noradrenaline** (also called **norepinephrine**). This is a major neurotransmitter which affects emotion. It heightens emergency reactions, the **'fight or flight'** syndrome.

2 The structure of the brain

The brain, together with the spinal cord, makes up the central nervous system. The spinal cord runs through the spine and connects to the peripheral nervous system. This controls reflexes (involuntary actions).

The brain is a collection of organs, each with a special responsibility, and each at a different level of sophistication.

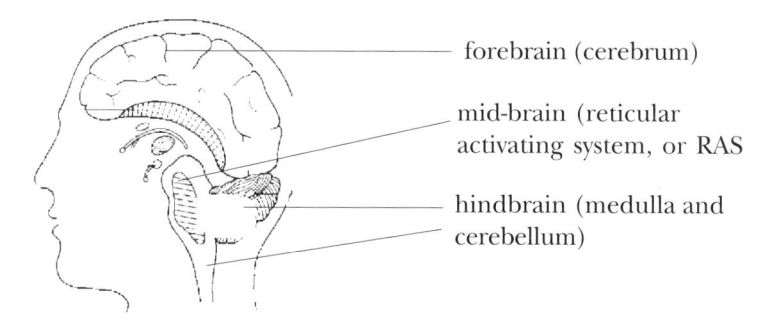

- forebrain (cerebrum)
- mid-brain (reticular activating system, or RAS)
- hindbrain (medulla and cerebellum)

(adapted from N.Hayes and S.Orrell, 1993)

Most primitive parts - hindbrain (medulla and cerebellum): controls automatic functions (breathing, digestion, heartbeat).

More advanced parts - mid-brain (reticular activating system, or RAS): controls level of arousal and attention, including sleep.

Most advanced parts - forebrain (cerebrum): contains the **hypothalamus**, governing body movement; the **thalamus**, governing consciousness; and the **limbic system**, affecting emotion, aggression and motivation.

The cerebrum

(a) has two **hemispheres**, each dealing with information from the opposite side of the body;
(b) has four **lobes**: the frontal lobe (general management); parietal lobe (concerned with motor control); temporal lobe (sensory capacities); occipital lobe (containing visual cortex);
(c) is covered by the **cortex**, a thin outer layer controlling perception, learning and memory, motor functions, production and understanding of language.

The function of each area of the cortex is still being discovered, including some specific language centres (angular gyrus, Wernicke's area, Broca's area).

3 Studying the brain

Psychologists study the brain because they believe that the mind and brain are inseparable and affect each other.

Methods of studying the brain include:

1 *observing brain-damaged patients* - not very reliable as there is often no clear indication what damage the brain has sustained. The damage is not sufficiently localised.

2 *surgical interference* - lesioning (cutting through tissue) or ablation (destroying tissue). This interference is highly localised and it is therefore assumed to be related to any subsequent changes in behaviour.

3 *recording brain reactions* - using micro-electrodes, ECGs, or brain scans.

4 Empirical studies

Psychologists most famous for studying the brain and its functions include *Sperry, Myers, Gazzaniga, Blakemore, Ornstein* and *Gooch.*

Myers and Sperry (1952) showed that the two halves of the brain acted as two brains if the corpus callosum joining the two hemispheres was cut.

Gazzaniga and Sperry (1967) reported that the two hemispheres seemed to have different functions. The left hemisphere seems dominant in terms of language, mathematical activities and tasks involving formal logic. The right hemisphere seems dominant in terms of visual-spatial understanding and also object identification.

Ornstein developed this theme (1974) saying that the left hemisphere was dominant in formal logic, involving numbers and words, while the right hemisphere was dominant in intuition, insight formation and creative thinking.

Blakemore (1984) showed that different cells in the brain can fire at different strengths, depending on the strength of the incoming stimulus.

Gooch (1980) suggested that if one hemisphere is out of order, the other hemisphere will adapt to make up for the functions that are lost. He argued that if this were the case, complete hemispherectomies (removal of whole hemisphere) might be a way of dealing with brain damage.

5 Evaluation

It is very tempting to speak about the brain and the mind as two separate things. Studies suggest that the mind has a physiological foundation - that is, what we think is influenced by the state of the brain. This view, however, is reductionist (reducing things to their component parts), suggesting that the mind exists only because the brain does. Look at Unit 11 and compare some of the ideas there.

We must also remember that the brain is the least understood organ of the body, and even less is understood about the mind. People working in artificial intelligence at the moment are offering some very interesting ideas here (see Unit 11).

6 Summary

How do we understand the workings of our brain? How do the workings of the brain affect the workings of our minds? Are the two separable?

To understand the way in which the emotions work, it is necessary to understand the structure of the brain and the functions of its different parts.

1 the nervous system

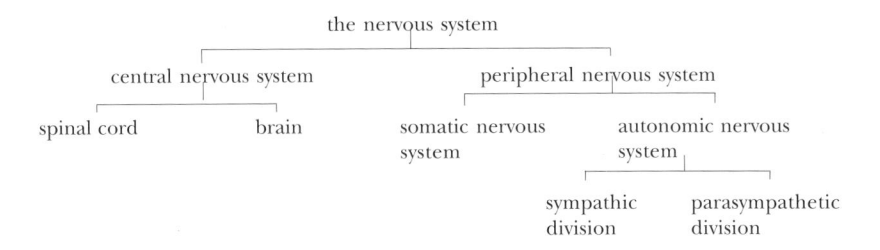

```
                    the nervous system
                    ┌──────────┴──────────┐
         central nervous system    peripheral nervous system
         ┌────────┴────────┐       ┌────────┴────────┐
    spinal cord         brain   somatic nervous   autonomic nervous
                                    system             system
                                                  ┌──────┴──────┐
                                              sympathetic  parasympathetic
                                               division        division
```

2 parts of the brain

    the hindbrain contains the medulla and cerebellum
    the mid-brain contains the reticular activating system (RAS)
    the forebrain (cerebrum) contains the hypothalamus, the thalamus, and the limbic system

The cerebrum	has two hemispheres
	has four lobes
	is covered by the cortex

3 Ways of studying the brain
observing brain-damaged patients
surgical interference
recording brain reactions

4 Theorists
Sperry, Myers, Gazzaniga, Ornstein, Blakemore, Gooch

7 Now ⟹ Over to you...

1 *Fill in the missing words*

The nervous system is divided into .... parts, the c............... n............... s....................... and the p....................... n....................... s....................... The CNS consists of the s....................... c....................... and the b..............., while the peripheral nervous system consists of the s....................... n....................... s....................... and the a....................... n....................... s........................ The autonomic nervous system sub-divides into the s........................ division and the p........................ division.

2 *Match the two halves of the sentences*

(a) The sympathetic division   (i)   slows reactions down
(b) The parasympathetic division   (ii) speeds reactions up

3 *Match the neurone with its function*

(a) connector neurones   (i) carry information from sense organs of the body to the brain and spinal cord
(b) sensory neurones   (ii) carry information from the brain and spinal cord to the muscles of the body, affecting movement
(c) motor neurones   (iii) carry information from one cell to another

4 *From the list of words, choose three words that refer to parts of the brain*

hindbrain, retrograde amnesia, interference, proximity, mid-brain, mnemonics, forebrain, cues, organisation, gradient of texture

5 *Unscramble the names of some famous psychologists who have studied the brain*

Rrepsy, Yerms, Ganiazazg, Steornin, Eblkeorma, Hcogo

7 Written exercises

1 What are the main branches of the nervous system and what are their functions?
2 What are the three kinds of neurones and what are their functions?
3 What effect has noradrenaline on the body and on the emotions?
4 What are the parts of the brain and what are their functions?
5 What are the main methods of studying the brain?

8 Topics for discussion

1 Why should psychologists study the brain?

2 What are some ethical considerations in studying the brain?

3 Do you consider that the brain and mind are inseparable or are they independent of each other?

4 Does our physical state necessarily influence our mental state? Can we control our physiological reactions through mental power, for example, through imaging or meditation or hypnosis (see Unit 13)?

9 Need to know

- Can you identify and name the different parts of the brain and their functions, as mentioned in this unit?
- Can you identify the three different kinds of neurones and specify their functions?
- Can you say what effects noradrenaline has on the body?
- Can you describe the main methods of studying the brain?
- Can you name all the psychologists mentioned in this unit and describe their work?
- Can you give a critical evaluation of their work?

10 Suggestions for coursework

1 Carry out an investigation on yourself or on a friend into the effects of physiological state on ability to do simple tasks. For example, try memorising a list of words, or doing complicated calculations when you or your friend are fresh and alert (possibly at 9 a.m.) Then try a similar task when you are tired (possibly at 9 p.m.) Keep a record of the successful number of tries.

More challenging studies

1 Work with a friend in studying cerebral dominance. Sit facing the friend across a table, with a fairly complex drawing in front of you. Place a clean sheet of paper at the end of the drawing, away from you, and draw the figure upside-down, so that it is the right way up for your friend. Do this first with your favourite hand, and then with your less favourite. Exchange roles, and ask your friend to do the same. Keep a record of accuracy, for example, by tallying the number of correct figures that you drew. Can you reach any conclusions from your study about the effects of cerebral dominance?

Unit Nine
Emotion – arousal and stress

This unit deals with the questions

Why do we feel emotions?
What theories help us to understand why we feel emotions?

Emotion and physiological processes seem to be connected to and dependent on each other. Psychologists disagree about whether emotion causes physiological reactions or vice versa: that is, do we feel the emotion first, and then our bodies change because of the emotion; or do our bodies change, making us to feel a particular emotion? Or is it an interaction of the two?

The main themes for this topic are

1 What happens in the body when we are aroused?
2 What is the nature of stress and what are its causes?
3 What theories of emotion are there?
4 How do we acquire emotions?

1 Emotion – physiological correlates

What happens in the body when we are aroused? Some psychologists say that the feeling of emotion, or arousal, is caused by an interaction between physiological aspects, which determine the **degree** of arousal, and cognitive aspects, which determine the **kind** of arousal.

Arousal is a general body state, and is caused by (a) external situational factors, such as how stimulating the context is, which make us interested or lethargic and so on; and (b) by the autonomic nervous system (ANS). People have different kinds of ANS: a lazy ANS means a lazy person; a very active ANS means a highly strung person. Arousal will also be affected by how much we are paying attention to what is going on, or how motivated we are, and other cognitive factors.

The Yerkes-Dodson Law

Level of arousal affects performance. There has to be a certain amount of arousal to get us going, but too much arousal can have a damaging effect.

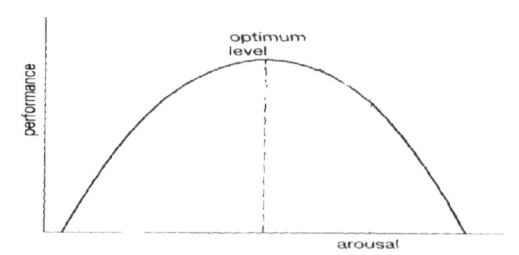

In the diagram you can see that there is an optimum level of performance and arousal. As the arousal level increases, performance drops off. You can perhaps notice this in yourself. When you have to do well at a task, a certain amount of 'keying up' gives you a necessary edge; but if you get too keyed up, you will start getting tense, and this will actually damage your performance.

The alarm reaction

In the 1920s, **Walter Cannon** coined the phrase '**fight or flight syndrome**', referring to the release of adrenalin into the blood stream by the sympathetic division of the ANS to help us cope with an emergency. Physiological changes are: heart beats faster, blood pressure increases, blood sugar level rises, saliva thickens, pupils dilate, hair stands on end. If all these responses are not needed, the parasympathetic division kicks in to slow everything down to normal again.

2 Stress: what is its nature and what are its causes?

Nature of stress

Selye (1946) investigated the body's long-term adaptation to stress - the **General Adaptation Syndrome** (GAS), when a high level of adrenalin is maintained. This can be damaging. *Solomon* (1963) showed that long-term exposure to stress had serious effects on the body's immune system.

Levine (1971) found that arousal can accelerate development in animals in early life; and some early exposure to stress can build up resistance in animals to stress in later life.

Brady (1958) showed that animals placed in a stressful decision-making situation suffered acute symptoms of stress (ulcers in executive monkeys).

Weiss (1972) found that rats could develop coping behaviours in stressful situations.

Causes of stress

There are three main causes of stress

> **environmental factors:** noise, pollution, etc.;
> **personal factors:** illness, bereavement, etc. (see *Holms and Rahe*, Recent Life Experience scale);
> **cognitive factors**: how we interpret the situation.

Friedman and Rosenman (1974) identified **Type A** and **Type B** persons. Type A individuals tend to be competitive, highly strung perfectionists. They show GAS symptoms and often suffer serious illness. Type B individuals tend to be more relaxed.

Treatments for stress

Drugs are used extensively.
Biofeedback helps the person to monitor and modify physical reactions.
Implosion therapy (flooding), **systematic desensitisation** and **modelling** are all techniques used in the treatment of phobias.
Meditation and imaging are techniques that help the person to recognise that healing lies in the self (see Unit 13).

3 Theories of emotion

Emotions are generally believed to consist of three parts:

> **the cognitive component** - knowledge about what led to the emotion;
> **the affective component** - the feeling of the emotion;
> **the behavioural component** - what we do when we are feeling an emotion.

We can measure the degree of arousal that the emotion generates by

> **galvanic skin response** (GSR) - biofeedback machines, polygraphs (lie detectors) and voice analysers work like this;
> **observing** people's facial expression and other body movements.

The James-Lange Theory

This theory says that we perceive the physiological state of our body, and this gives rise to the emotion. James says: *'We do not weep because we feel sorrow; we feel sorrow because we weep.'* An example of this is if you slip on the stairs, your heart lurches, you grab for the rail - only later do you feel fear.

James-Lange theory

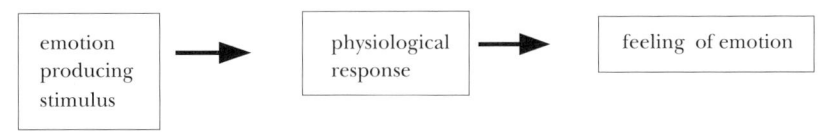

```
emotion            physiological        feeling of emotion
producing    →     response        →
stimulus
```

The Cannon-Bard Theory

This theory says that emotion and physiological reaction are separate things. Emotion is psychological; bodily reactions are physiological. The emotion we feel depends on how well we understand the situation that caused it.

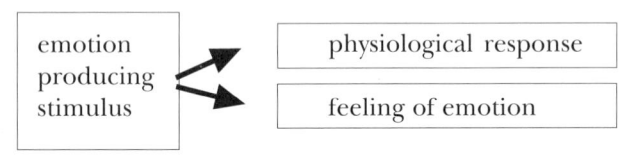

Cannon-Bard theory

```
emotion         →   physiological response
producing
stimulus        →   feeling of emotion
```

Schachter and Singer's Theory

This theory suggests a relationship between cognitive understanding of the social situation that produces the emotion and physiological factors: the cognitive determines the type of emotion felt, and the physiological determines its strength. This theory was supported by work carried out by **Valins and Hohmans**. The theory is probably the most popular today.

Schachter and Singer's theory

```
                    cognitive
                    factors
                   ↗         ↘
emotion                       emotion
producing                     experience
stimulus           
                   ↘         ↗
                    general
                    arousal/
                    physiological
                    response
```

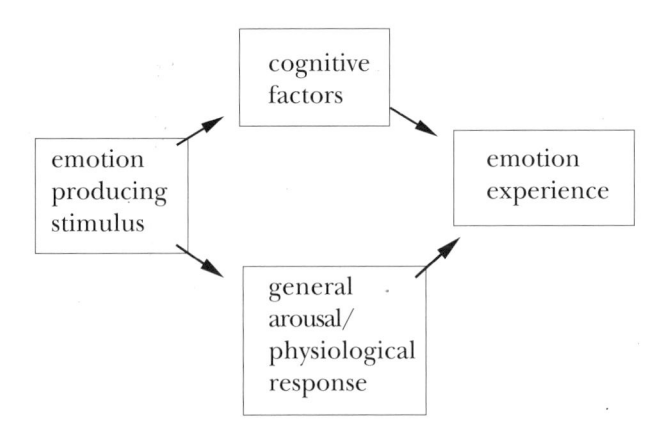

4 Acquisition of emotions

Some theories of how and why we acquire emotions include:

Behaviourist theories: see *Watson*'s conditioning of little Albert. He banged an iron bar behind little Albert's head while Albert was watching a rat. Not surprisingly, Albert came to fear rats.

Genetic inheritance: *Broadhurst* made rats afraid, then selectively bred high emotional rats and low emotional rats.

Innate factors: *Ekman et al.* found certain emotional expressions to be universal.

Early life exposure to stress: see *Levine's* work with rats. He found that handling in early life seemed to help rats to build up an emotional resistance to trauma in later life.

Maternal deprivation: see *Bowlby's* idea of affectionless psychopathy, an inability to relate to others or to develop a social conscience because of early life maternal deprivation.

Learned helplessness

Seligman showed that dogs seemed to learn that nothing they did had any effect in avoiding unpleasant events; they became passive and gave up.
Zimbardo demonstrated that dogs that had previous early-life exposure to stress did not suffer learned helplessness.

5 Evaluation

There seems to be general agreement amongst psychologists that physiological and cognitive responses are linked. Where a lot of disagreement lies is whether the physiological determines the cognitive response, or the other way round. You need to think this through for yourself. What is your real experience? Is there a case for an interactionist point of view, such as Schachter and Singer's?

Stress is another aspect that causes some disagreement amongst psychologists. There are different ideas about what causes stress, and whether this is linked to personality type. Some people seem to thrive on stress, while others suffer at a small amount of stress. Some educational practices are based on the idea that a certain amount of stress is useful for children; and some professions build in stress training as part of their personnel development programmes.

What do you feel are the most important factors in stress? A lot of 'modern' ailments are stress related. How can stress be relieved?

6 Summary

Why do we feel emotions? What theories help us to understand why we feel emotions?

1 Emotion - physiological correlates
Factors involved in producing emotion are degree of arousal, kind of arousal, type of ANS.
The Yerkes-Dodson Law links level of arousal with performance.
The alarm reaction - 'fight or flight' - helps the body to prepare for emergencies.

2 Stress
Stress is a major factor in our lives. Emotion can easily turn to stress.
Nature of stress: can be damaging, but can also be useful in building up resistance in later life;
Causes of stress: environmental factors, personal factors, cognitive factors;
Treatments for stress: drugs, biofeedback, implosion therapy, meditation and imaging.

3 Theories of emotion
The traditional view is that an emotion has three parts: the cognitive, affective and behavioural components.
> **The James-Lange Theory** states that physiological factors cause the emotion.
> **The Cannon-Bard Theory** states that emotional and physiological responses are separate.
> **The Schachter and Singer Theory** states that there is interaction between emotion and physiological factors, which are both influenced by an appreciation of the social situation.

4 Acquisition of emotions
Theories of how emotions are acquired include
> **Behaviourist theories**
> **Genetic inheritance**
> **Innate factors**
> **Early life experiences**
> **Maternal deprivation**
> **Learned helplessness**

7 Now → Over to you...

1 *Write the words 'performance' and 'arousal' in the correct place on the diagram, and then draw in the curve*

2 *Complete the sentence:* The famous phrase, 'We do not weep because we feel sorrow; we feel sorrow because we weep' applies to..
....
....

3 *Unscramble the names of three psychologists who worked with animals to show the effects of stress:* Evleni, Dyrab, Sseiw

4 *From the list, choose three factors that are the main causes of stress*

behaviourist factors, environmental factors, interference factors, memory factors, personal factors, maternal deprivation factors, cognitive factors, fight or flight factors

5 *Complete the sentences*

Type A persons have the following characteristics: ....
....
Type B persons have the following characteristics: ....
....

6 *Match the theory with the description*

(a) The James-Lange theory   (i)   states that there is interaction between emotion and physiological factors, which are both influenced by an appreciation of the social situation

(b) The Cannon-Bard theory   (ii)   states that physiological factors cause the emotion

(c) Schachter and Singer's theory   (iii)   states that emotional and physiological responses are separate

8 Written exercises

1 What physiological changes take place when we are aroused?
2 Explain how the sympathetic and parasympathetic divisions of the ANS work together to keep the body stable.
3 What are some of the causes of stress, and how can they be relieved?
4 How can emotion be measured?
5 What are the three main theories of emotion? Write brief notes on each.
6 How are emotions acquired?

9 Topics for discussion

1 What do you think is the relationship between the cognitive and physiological factors in emotion?

2 What commonsense advice could you offer to a friend who has recently experienced some emotional upset, advising him or her how to cope with the situation?

3 Do you think that humans also learn helplessness? What might society do to encourage people to be in control of their own lives?

10 Need to know

➭ Can you say what some of the physiological correlates of emotion are?

➭ Can you explain the workings of the Yerkes-Dodson Law?

➭ Can you describe how the 'fight or flight' syndrome works?

➭ Can you name the major causes of stress? Can you say how stress might be relieved?

➭ Can you outline the theories of (a) James-Lange; (b) Cannon-Bard; (c) Schachter and Singer?

➭ Can you say what theories explain how emotions are acquired?

11 Suggestions for coursework

Note

It is very difficult to link coursework with the ideas in this unit because of the ethical issues which would be raised. You could do some of these studies only if the participants know in advance the purpose of the study, agree to take part, and understand that they can withdraw at any time.

1 Carry out an observational study of people in an emotional or stressful situation, such as at a railway station, or in a dentist's waiting room, or at a supermarket checkout. What kind of behaviour do they show? Is this behaviour any different from behaviour in a non-stressful environment? You will need to compare the group you observe with another group in a non-stressful situation, such as in a park, or in a restaurant. Devise categories of behaviour.

2 Conduct an investigation to test the hypothesis, 'Too much arousal can interfere with performance'. Relate your findings, if appropriate, to the Yerkes-Dodson law.

> ✳ **REMEMBER** ✳ You cannot conduct an investigation where participants are deliberately made to feel anxious.

More challenging studies

1 Investigate the Yerkes-Dodson Law. Arrange two groups, Group A and Group B (unrelated samples design). Ask Group A to undertake a fairly challenging mental task, such as doing complex calculations. Give them a strict time-limit, but not so strict that it is going to be stressful. Negotiate this with the group. Record their scores on the task. Ask Group B to do the same task, but explain that they are going to do this under pressure. (Remind them that they have the right to refuse or withdraw. *See note above.*) Give them a very tight time limit. Record their scores on the task. Compare the scores of Group A and Group B.

2 Factors other than stress can explain differences in performance. Conduct the investigation outlined above, but ask Group A to work with people watching them, while Group B would work without an audience. The time limit would be equal for both groups. What conclusions could you draw? You could relate this study also to audience effects (see Unit 19).

3 Carry out a survey into what people think are the most common factors that cause stress. You could extend this study and link it to personality type, to see if the idea of Type A and Type B personalities is valid. You will need to include some kind of personality self-assessment of the people who are involved in answering your questions. (Note: you must not attempt to conduct a personality assessment test yourself, even using one of the popular 'Know your own personality' type of books. *There are serious ethical issues here.*)

Unit Ten
Language

This unit deals with the questions

What is the nature of language?
How do we acquire language?
How do we use language?

There is a lot of disagreement amongst psychologists and linguists about

1 the nature of language - is it specific only to humans, or can chimpanzees, dolphins and other animals 'speak' to each other?
2 what 'language' means - is it something different from communication?
3 how we acquire language - is the capacity for language innate or learned?

Traditionally, language has been described as having three different aspects:

phonological	- the sound system
syntactic	- the order in which words go
semantic	- the meaning of words and sentences

The main themes for this topic are

1 The relationship between language and thinking
2 Theories of language acquisition
3 The uses of language
4 Animals and language

1 The relationship between language and thinking

What is the relationship between language and thinking? Do we need language in order to think, or do we need thought in order to have language? There are three points of view here.

1 Language encourages thinking

Behaviourist views argue that language determines thought.

Watson (1913), for example, believed that sub-vocal activity was essential to thinking.

Linguistic relativity hypothesis

There is a strong and a weak view of this hypothesis. ***Sapir and Whorf*** said that, in order to have a concept, we must first have the language to describe that concept. Language determines thinking, perception and memory. If we haven't got the words to describe something, we cannot think about that thing. It can't exist because the language to describe it doesn't exist. This is the strong version of the hypothesis. The weak version says that language affects thinking, perception and memory, but does not determine them.

Elaborated and restricted codes

Bernstein (1961) said that people use a particular kind of language depending on their social status and context. Middle and upper class people tend to use an **elaborated code**; lower class people tend to use a **restricted code**. This view has been heavily criticised. *Labov* (1970) showed that it didn't matter whether the language used fitted in with traditional views of social stereotypes. The language itself was rich and meaningful, and in no way reflected the intelligence or other abilities of the speaker.

Dialect

People tend to think (like Bernstein) that the kind of language we use in social situations reflects our level of intelligence. *Rosenthal* (1966) and *Meichenbaum* (1966) showed how teachers behaved differently towards pupils with different dialects. The teachers tended to be more sympathetic and pay more attention to children who spoke something like 'BBC style English' than towards children who spoke with accents or dialects. The pupils' achievements reflected this. Those who had more attention did better than those who did not (the **self-fulfilling prophecy**).

2 Thinking encourages language

Piaget believed that intellectual development involved a whole system of cognitive operations. Children acquire knowledge of the world through play and exploration. They actively construct reality through interaction with the environment. For Piaget, language was not an end-product of thinking, but a tool that could be used to help thinking. He believed that thinking exists before language, but language helps the development of thinking. The child is saying its thought aloud, and so developing its language, its thinking and its understanding of reality. Later the child will see language as a useful tool to help communication and problem-solving.

Bruner (see below at 2) was very much influenced by Piaget, and also thought that language was vital for the development of thinking.

3 Language and thinking as separate and independent

Vygotsky (1962) believed, like Piaget, that children could think before they could use language. He believed that language, along with everything else, develops as a result of social interaction. For Vygotsky, the social element is most important. Language is acquired through, because of, and for social communication. This view also applies to thinking. What and how the child thinks is decided through interaction and conversation with other people. For Vygotsky, language and thinking develop separately, always in relation to other people, until about the age of 2, when they come together and help each other, and become part of the overall process of development within a social framework.

2 How is language acquired and developed?

Stages of language development

Many psychologists agree that there is a definite timetable for the development of language in children, and it appears that all children go through various phases of linguistic development, something like this:

1-4 months	general noises, turning to cooing
5-9 months	babbling
9-18 months	exploring phonemes (units of sound joined together)
1-1½ years	production of one and two-word phrases
1½-2½ years	telegraphic speech
2½-5/6 years	development of grammar and syntax

Theories of language acquisition and development

Behaviourist theories

Skinner (1957) said that language was **verbal behaviour.** It was learned in the same way as other behaviour, through conditioning. A specific stimulus produced a particular response. Children learned language by imitation and habit formation. They heard a sentence, and would produce another sentence like it, substituting vocabulary where necessary.

So	'The	cat	sat	on	the	mat'
could become	'The	cat	sat	on	the	chair'
or	'The	dog	sat	on	the	floor'

The development of language was largely a matter of trial and error. The child explored which word or structure fitted best and was understood.

Nativist theories

Chomsky (1957) criticised the behaviourist view. He said that the ability for language was innate, in the same way that the ability to see, hear and walk is innate. It is a natural function of the human species to produce language. In his early work, Chomsky proposed a **Language Acquisition Device,** a kind of black box, which contained the blueprint for knowledge of language and language production. Chomsky distinguished two levels of language: **competence** - the underlying system of rules for language that every person has; and **performance**, the use of those rules in real-life situations. Chomsky's work did a lot to discredit the behaviourist approach to language acquisition and development, as well as have a lasting effect on thinking in linguistics and psychology. He was always concerned with *how* we acquire and develop language, not why.

Cognitive theories

Piaget (see above) said that children 'discover' language and find that they can use it as a tool to help thinking and, later, communication. Piaget was more concerned with *why* we acquire and develop language.

Vygotsky (see above) felt that language and thinking existed separately until about the age of two, when they came together as part of the general development of the child.

Bruner had a particular view of development, and said that there are three ways in which we come to understand what is going on around us. These are the enactive, the iconic and the symbolic (see Unit 6). This is also the order in which they develop in the child. The enactive mode is to do with how we perceive our own actions. The child will remember what it feels like to do certain things. The iconic mode is to do with our visual knowledge and the mental images we build up. The child will perceive the world in terms of pictures. The symbolic mode refers to linguistic representation. The child can put words to its pictures and physical experiences of the world. Language is vital here to enable the child to turn physical experience into words to communicate its understanding. Language is therefore central to thinking.

Social theories

Brown (1973) emphasised the social dimension of language.

Jill and Peter de Villiers said that conversation between adults and children was something like a teaching-learning situation, and it accelerates language development.

Stern (1977) and *Snow* (1977) also showed how conversation between parents and children helps children to use and understand language.

3 How is language used?

There are several perspectives to language use. This is better found in theories of linguistics, but there are some important implications for psychological study as well.

1 The first obvious use of language is as **communication**, and there is a lot of research going on into the dynamics of communication. Studies are being conducted, for example, into the 'rules' of communication, such as who speaks and when, and how we take turns to hold centre-stage. There is also a lot of interesting research into 'the politics of discourse' such as who is allowed to speak and who is allowed to be heard, and who decides these things.

2 Another use of language is in helping us to study the mind (**psycholinguistics**). In this, the operations of language give us an idea about the state of mind/brain of the person using the language. Chomsky's work is significant here.

3 Language is also helping us to understand the workings of **computers**, and giving us insights into the workings of the human mind/brain. In Artificial Intelligence, some people see the computer as a mind/brain, or at least as representing the workings of the human mind/brain. By studying the way that computers work, and matching that with the way that language works, psychologists are coming to a better understanding of the way the human mind/brain works.

These issues are not part of GCSE work, but we are mentioning them here to point out what is happening in current research into language use.

4 Animals and language

The major point here is whether language is species-specific - that is, is it only humans who use language, or do other non-human animals have language?

There is little doubt that non-human animals communicate, but whether or not they use language systems to communicate is far harder to say. So is the question of whether any communication system used by animals can be called language.

A number of studies have been carried out on chimps, to see whether or not they could develop something the same as human language. Sarah, Washoe, Koko, Kanzi, and Nim Chimpsky are the most famous.

General conclusions about teaching language to chimps are:

1 Chimps can develop an impressive vocabulary using sign language - up to 400 signs (Koko).
2 They can understand spoken instructions and act on them.
3 They can hold a conversation in sign language and can start a conversation.
4 They can refer to events in the past.
5 They can use abstract concepts and generalise.

However, all studies so far have looked at aspects of language **production**. There is still no evidence that chimps have linguistic **competence** - that is, that they are 'programmed' to acquire and use language. There is also the big question whether it is ethically right to try to teach chimps language.

5 Evaluation

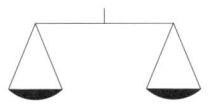

The debate about the nature of language, how it is acquired, and how it is used, continues today as hotly as ever it did in the 1950s and 60s. There is a lot of disagreement about whether language is innate or whether it is learned. Few psychologists today would take the extreme view of the early behaviourists, saying that language was learned by stimulus-response. Not all psychologists would agree entirely with Chomsky, that language is an innate system, although Chomsky's work opened up a whole new way of thinking about language and its acquisition.

The debate about the use of language by animals has a very high public profile at the moment. A number of ethologists (people observing animals in natural habitats) believe that some animal species have developed their own form of communication. Some scientists say that this is 'language' while others are more cautious and say that animals have 'communication systems'.

The debate of trying to teach language to chimps also rages. At the moment, there is interesting research going on with second-generation chimps who have been taught American Sign Language. The chimps are now teaching it to their young without any prompting from their human minders.

6 Summary

What is the nature of language? How do we acquire language? How do we use language?

1 The relationship between language and thinking

There are three views:
(a) **language encourages thinking** (*Watson, Sapir and Whorf, Bernstein*)
  Aspects of this view are
    the linguistic relativity hypothesis: *Sapir and Whorf* said that the language for a concept must exist before we can have the concept;
    elaborated and restricted codes: *Bernstein* said that language ability depends on what social class people belong to, and that there are particular codes for different social classes. This view was criticised by people like ***Labov***.
(b) **thinking encourages language** (*Piaget, Bruner*)
(c) **thinking and language are separate and independent** (*Vygotsky*)

2 How is language acquired and developed?

Language development seems to follow a regular timetable in children.

3 Theories of language acquisition and development

There are four sets of theories of language acquisition and development:
  behaviourist theories (*Skinner*)
  nativist theories (*Chomsky*)
  cognitive theories (*Piaget, Vygotsky, Bruner*)
  social theories (*Brown, Jill and Peter de Villiers, Stern, Snow*)

4 How is language used?

There is a lot of interesting research going on into the various uses of language, including the communication function of language, study of the mind/brain, and work with computers.

5 Animals and language

The debate continues about whether animals can - and should - use language systems to communicate.

7 Now Over to you...

1 *Match the word with the description*

(a) phonology   (i)   the order in which words go
(b) syntax   (ii) the meaning of words and sentences
(c) semantics   (iii) the sound system

2 *In the following sentences, fill the blanks with the correct name from this list*

Sapir and Whorf, Bernstein, Skinner, Chomsky, Piaget, Vygotsky

(a) .... said that we could not have a concept unless we had the language to describe the concept.
(b) .... said that language was verbal behaviour and was learned through stimulus-response.
(c) ....said that language and thinking were separate, but came together when the child was about two years old.
(d) .... said that language depended on social class.
(e) .... said that language helped thinking to develop.
(f) .... said that language was part of our natural inheritance, the same as walking, seeing and hearing.

3 *Complete the sentence*

Trying to teach chimps to use language could be seen as unethical, because..............
....
....

8 Written exercises

1 What are (a) the linguistic relativity hypothesis; (b) elaborated and restricted codes?
2 Describe the differences between the work of Watson, Piaget and Vygotsky, with reference to the relationship between language and thinking.
3 With reference to language acquisition and development, what are the major differences between the views of Skinner and Chomsky?
4 What are Bruner's three modes of representation, and why are they significant for his views on the development of language?
5 What evidence is there that chimpanzees can learn language?

9   Topics for discussion

1. Do you think that the way we speak reflects our intelligence?

2. Do you think language is something that we are born with or something that we learn? Or is it a mixture of both?

3. What are your opinions about trying to teach chimps language?

9   Need to know

- Can you explain what the linguistic relativity hypothesis means?
- Can you describe the work of Bernstein, and elaborated and restricted codes?
- Can you describe the different approaches to the relationship between language and thinking?
- Can you outline the main differences of opinion between Skinner and Chomsky?
- Can you outline the major differences in the behaviourist, nativist, cognitive, and social approaches to language acquisition and development?
- Can you comment critically (and unemotionally) on work with chimps to investigate language acquisition and development in humans?
- Can you name all the psychologists mentioned in this unit, and give a description of their work?

9 Suggestions for coursework

1 Conduct an investigation to test the hypothesis that there are differences between male/female linguistic abilities by getting a group of males and a group of females to unscramble sentences in a given time limit. You could vary the theme and investigate the idea that 12 and 15 year olds also have different linguistic abilities.

2 Carry out a survey into public opinion of the use of trying to teach chimps language. Find out if people think it is a worthwhile activity, or if it is a waste of time. As an extension of this study, you might test public opinion on the ethical issue of trying to teach chimps language.

More challenging studies

1 Carry out an observational study of a child/children to investigate language development. Listen to them speaking, and record instances of the type of speech they use - cooing/babbling/telegraphic speech. Relate their ability to produce language with the idea of a 'timetable' for language development.

2 Conduct an investigation to test the hypothesis that the kind of language used by males and females reinforces traditional gender-role stereotypes.

Unit Eleven
Thinking, problem solving and intelligence

This unit deals with the questions

What is the nature of thinking and intelligence?
How do we acquire thinking and intelligence?
How do we use thinking and intelligence?

Although we use the words 'thinking' and 'intelligence' freely and in a taken-for-granted way, they are among the most difficult concepts to define. Psychologists disagree particularly about what we are doing when we say we are thinking, or what it means to be intelligent; and whether thinking and intelligence are particular skills or general abilities. There are many opinions about questions like these:

What, if any, is the difference between thinking and intelligence?
What theories help us understand what we are doing when we are thinking?
Can we improve our thinking and intelligence?

The main themes of this topic are:

1 Can we define thinking and intelligence?
2 What theories help us to understand how we think?
3 How is intelligence acquired?
4 How do we use our thinking and intelligence?

1 Definitions

There is a lot of debate about the nature of thinking and intelligence, and also a lot of overlap in concepts and definitions. Can all cognitive activity be called thinking? Are we thinking only when we are problem solving? Is all problem-solving intelligent? Is intelligence a thing or a process?

Some basic issues

There are a number of definitions of thinking:

Osgood (1953) says thinking is 'the internal representation of events'.

Freud (1900) says thinking happens from the need to satisfy biological urges.

Piaget sees thinking as the development of schemata through assimilation, accommodation and adaptation.

Boden (1987) believes that all thinking involves problem solving.

There are a number of definitions of intelligence:

Eysenck believes that intelligence can be measured (the psychometric approach).

Gardner (1983) believes that we have multiple intelligences, such as musical intelligence, visual-spatial intelligence, and so on, along with the more traditional numerical-verbal intelligence.

Thinking and intelligence are linked in the sense that intelligence is usually seen as a qualitative aspect of thinking - but this is not always the case. For example, what if I am an autistic person with highly developed intelligence in one area such as drawing? Would I have 'limited intelligence' in other areas? Would I be 'thinking'?

2 Theories

How do we think?

The following studies provide empirical evidence to help us understand what happens when we are thinking.

Trial-and-error: *Thorndike* (1898) said that animals learned through trial and error.

Insight learning: *Köhler* (1925) and other Gestalt psychologists said that we stick with a problem until various possible solutions come together.

Cognitive styles: *Hudson* (1966) identified the concepts of convergent and divergent thinking, something like the difference between thinking along traditional lines, and thinking up new ideas and new ways of thinking.

Lateral thinking: *De Bono* developed this idea, which is also about developing new ways of thinking.

Learning sets: *Harlow* explored the idea of 'learning to learn'.

Luchins (1942) took this idea further. The successful development of learning sets helps overcome **functional fixedness** (what the Gestalt psychologists called *Einstellung*), where we might get stuck in one way of thinking, and need to 'loosen up' our thinking to find new possibilities.

Models of thinking

Work in **Artificial Intelligence** is aimed at helping us to understand how the brain operates. This is based on the idea that a computer works in the same way as a human brain works. This may not be so! The 'strong' version of AI says that computers actually think. The 'weak' version says that the computer enables us to test hypotheses about the way the human brain works.

3 How is intelligence acquired? (But what is intelligence?)

The nature-nurture debate

Historically, there are two views that come out of the nature-nurture debate.

The nativists (nature) believe that intelligence is innate, and inherited through genetic transmission.

The empiricists (nurture) believe that intelligence is one specific, or a combination of several general, skills which are acquired through experience and interactions.

Galton (a nativist) believed that intelligence was inherited. His work led to the study of **eugenics** - that people of so-called inferior qualities should be prevented from having families.

Burt developed the idea that intelligence is inherited in his work on intelligence testing.

Shields (1962) however found no concrete evidence for this view in his study of MZ(identical) and DZ(fraternal) twins; nor did Skodak and Skeels (1945) in their studies of adopted children.

Can intelligence be measured?

Binet (an empiricist) believed that intelligence could develop through experience and education. He developed IQ tests to identify children who needed help in traditional academic subjects. The idea of IQ testing has changed in modern times, and IQ tests are now used as measures of ability rather than diagnostic tools (see ***Eysenck and Jensen,*** and ***Eysenck and Keanes***).

There is a lot of debate about the value of IQ tests. It seems that the only thing about IQ tests that psychologists do agree upon is that they teach people how to do IQ tests!

4 How do we use our thinking and intelligence?

Concept formation

We use our thinking to form concepts about the world which help us to make sense of it. Concepts are ideas about how things may be identified and grouped.

Formation of schemata

Piaget suggested that we organise our concepts as **schemata**. Adaptation to the environment would involve the successful development of multiple schemata.

5 Evaluation

This is a really tricky area, because what we say about thinking and intelligence depends squarely on what we think they are - if we see them as structures or processes. Is intelligence simply a degree of thinking? What qualifies as thinking? Who qualifies as intelligent? You will need to make up your own mind about this, but, as always, be prepared to quote psychological studies which support your own thinking. You might come to the conclusion that there is no such thing as intelligence - that it is a convenient label to describe certain ways of thinking! Provided you can defend your position with reasoned argument, you are fully entitled to your own opinion.

6 Summary

1 Definitions of thinking and intelligence

Thinking is a cognitive activity; many psychologists maintain that it involves problem solving.
Intelligence may be seen as a qualitative dimension, but it may also be seen as

        a specific ability *(Eysenck)*
        multiple intelligences (*Gardner*)

2 Theories that show different kinds of thinking

Trial-and-error *(Thorndike)*
Insight learning *(Köhler)*
Cognitive styles *(Hudson)*
Lateral thinking *(De Bono)*
Learning sets *(Harlow, Luchins)*

Models that show how thinking might happen
Artificial Intelligence: weak and strong versions

3 How is intelligence acquired?

The nature-nurture debate says:
intelligence develops naturally - the nature side of the debate: **Galton, Burt**
intelligence is learned - the nurture side of the debate: **Binet**

Can intelligence be measured?
Binet developed IQ tests, which are used today in ways not originally intended.

4 How do we use our thinking and intelligence?

- in the development of concept formation
- in the development of schemata (**Piaget**)

7   Now ⟹ over to you...

1 *In the following passage choose the correct version from the options given*

There is/there is not a lot of discussion about what intelligence and thinking are.
Most/not many psychologists believe that thinking involves problem-solving, but **everyone/not everyone** agrees about this.
Piaget/Freud believes that thinking is the development of schemata through assimilation, accommodation and adaptation, while **Piaget/Freud** believes that thinking happens from the need to satisfy biological urges.
Eysenck/Gardner believes that intelligence can be measured, while **Eysenck/Gardner** believes that intelligence is not just one thing but a whole series of different kinds of intelligence.
It really **is/is not** a difficult subject.

2 *Match the theory with the theorist*

    (a) trial and error   (i)   De Bono
    (b) insight learning   (ii)   Harlow
    (c) cognitive styles   (iii)   Thorndike
    (d) learning sets   (iv)   Hudson
    (e) lateral thinking   (v)   Köhler

3 *Complete the following sentences*

(a) Galton believed..
(b) Burt believed ....
(c) Shields found ....
(d) Binet invented ....

4 *Fill in the missing words*

Piaget said that we organise our c.................... as s.................... Concepts help us to make sense of the world by organising our ideas about it.

8 Written exercises

1 Define thinking and intelligence, to explain how you understand them.
2 What is the difference between the approaches of Eysenck and Gardner in the study of intelligence?
3 What is the use of intelligence tests? How are they used in society today?
4 Can studies in Artificial Intelligence help us to understand how the human mind/brain works?
5 What are the differences in approach between the nativists and the empiricists in the study of thinking and intelligence?

9 Topics for discussion

1 What do you think intelligence is? Is it a thing which can be measured, or is it a process that develops along with other processes?

2 How would you describe someone who is intelligent?

3 What kinds of thinking do you do? Would you call all of your mental activity thinking? What about when you are day-dreaming? Is that thinking, too?

{4} Would you say that autistic people can be described as intelligent? Give very clear reasons for your answer.

10 Need to know

▱ Can you give a definition for thinking and intelligence?

▱ Can you name all the psychologists mentioned in this unit, and clearly describe their work?

▱ Can you critically evaluate different approaches to theories of thinking and intelligence?

▱ Can you say how we use thinking and intelligence?

11 Suggestions for coursework

1 Carry out a survey into the use of intelligence tests. Gather people's opinion about their usefulness or their limitations. You could use an attitude scale here, as well as ask direct questions.

2 Devise a series of verbal and spatial tasks to investigate the hypothesis that there is a difference between male and female verbal and spatial abilities.

Note: You must not attempt to measure the intelligence of people - not even using the popular published books of 'Know your own IQ', etc. There are very strong ethical reasons for this.

More challenging studies

1 Carry out an investigation into the possibly different ways that males and females think while studying. Ask a group of females and a group of males to keep a record of how much time they spend problem solving, using imagery, daydreaming, using lateral thinking, and using trial and error over an hour's study time. Compare the results and draw conclusions about the possibly different cognitive styles of males and females.

2 Carry out an investigation into the ways that people think. Ask individuals to work out one of the puzzles below, and then ask them to talk through what they are thinking. You might ask them to tape record their comments. Note the number of instances they use different kinds of thinking: you could use categories of behaviour such as 'creative thinking', 'lateral thinking', 'formal thinking', 'insight learning'. Tally the number of times they engage in the various mental activities. Time how long it takes them to solve the puzzle. Draw some possible conclusions between thinking style and problem solving ability.

Puzzles

The eight-puzzle: A 3 x 3 matrix containing the numbers 1-8, with one vacant square, must be moved until the numbers are in order.

Change:

5	4	8
7	2	6
3		1

to:

1	2	3
4	5	6
7	8	

Scheerer's nine-dot problem:

Draw four continuous straight lines connecting all of the dots without lifting the pencil from the paper

Answer:

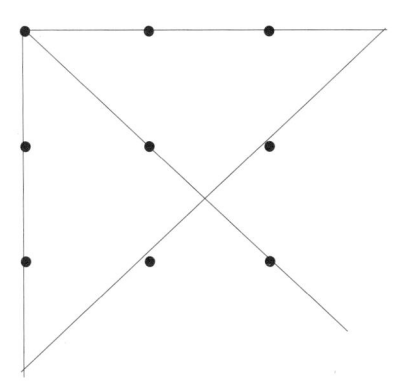

There are a number of good puzzle books available to give you lots of ideas.

Unit Twelve
Attention

This unit deals with the questions

**Why do we attend to some things and not to others?
What happens when we attend?**

Attention has to be selective. If we were to attend to everything that we sense, we would be swamped. We would constantly be aware of everything that was happening via our eyes, ears, nose, mouth, skin, and internal organs. Life would be intolerable. What factors operate, then, to decide what we attend to and what we ignore? What happens so that we attend to some things and ignore others?

Attention is bound up with perception. We attend to certain aspects and not others: this implies that we perceive them. We attend in order to act on certain bits of information or commit them to long-term memory.

The main themes of this topic are

1 Factors influencing attention
2 Ways of studying attention
3 Models of selective attention

1 Factors influencing attention

What we perceive will be influenced by personal and environmental factors, as well as the factors within the perceived object itself.

Personal and environmental factors (see also unit 2)

- such as -

perceptual set I will attend to something if I am ready to do so. If I am not ready it may go unnoticed.

expectation	I will attend to something if it is what I expect. If it is not, I may not perceive it.
primacy and recency effects	I will attend to things depending on where they are in the order of other things claiming my attention.
motivation	I will attend to things depending on how much I want to attend to them.
emotion	I will attend to things depending on the mood I am in. If I am happy, I might be alert; if I am miserable, I might be apathetic.
values	I will more likely attend to those things that I am in sympathy with than those that I don't find attractive.
level of arousal	I am more likely to attend to things if I am alert.
level of comfort	I am more likely to attend to things if I am comfortable
level of distraction	I am more likely to attend to things if I am not otherwise distracted.

Factors within the perceived object

- such as -

Is the perceived object familiar?	I will attend to my mother's voice but not a stranger's.
Is it personally meaningful?	I will attend to the mention of my own name.
Is it extraordinary?	I will attend to a very sudden loud noise.
Is it pleasant?	I will attend to a pleasing experience, and attempt to ignore an unpleasant one.

2 Ways of studying attention

The earliest attempts recorded in the psychological literature were by **Wilhelm Wundt** and the introspectionists, who studied their own mental processes. During the heyday of behaviourism and empirical approaches, introspection was not regarded as a very scientific way of doing psychology. Currently it is enjoying a comeback.

The most usual methods used today are: (1) **shadowing**; (2) **dual-task**.

Most studies have been done in auditory perception.

Shadowing

In this technique, message A is fed to the participant through headphones into one ear, and message B is fed into the other ear. The participant has to attend to and repeat only one message as it is played. This technique aims to examine how people select the information they want. Investigators who used this method include **Broadbent**, **Cherry**, **Moray**, **Triesman** (see below at 3).

Dual-task

In this technique, message A is fed into one ear, and message B is fed into the other (the same as in shadowing), but the participant is asked to attend to and perceive both messages. This technique aims to help us study people's capacity to attend to incoming information, that is, how much information they can attend to at any one time and if it is possible to attend to conflicting messages. Investigators who used this technique include Shaffer, Allport, Eysenck and Keanes.

3 Models of attention

Single channel models (filter models)

There are three major models by **Broadbent, Triesman,** and **Deutsch and Deutsch.** They all operate on the principle of a bottleneck, or filter. The difference between the three models is where the filter is supposed to be.

The idea of a filter is this. As noted above, we would be swamped if we attended to every piece of data that we sensed, so we filter out unnecessary data and keep only the data we want.

Broadbent's filter model

Triesman's attenuation model

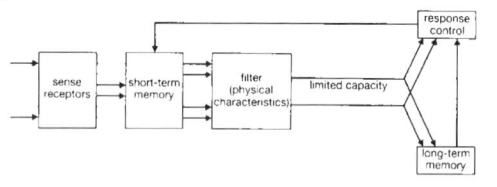

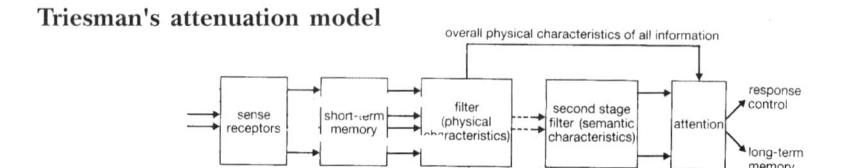

(diagrams adapted from N.Hayes and S.Orrell, 1993)

Deutsch and Deutsch's pertinence model (see also Norman's model)

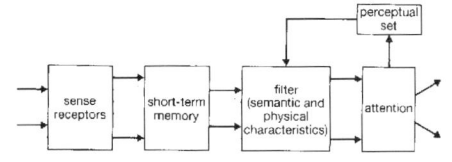

(adapted from N.Hayes and S.Orrell, 1993)

Challenges to the single-channel model

Kahnemann's limited capacity model

Kahnemann said that attention was limited by how much attention we were able, or prepared, to pay to something. He said that the mind had a **central processor** - a kind of decision-making centre - which decided how much mental energy could be given to a particular task. This depended on how tired we were, or how interesting the task was, or whether we wanted to pay attention to that task. This idea is something like when we have a limited amount of money to spend, and we decide where to spend it depending on a number of certain factors.

Neisser's active cycle model

Neisser felt that the idea of a single channel filter model did not explain how it is that we perceive. He believed that perception was a skill, and we could become better at it with practice. We learn how to perceive by actively exploring the world and building on our existing knowledge.

This is different from the filter model. Those models suggest that we filter unwanted information out. Neisser's model suggests that we explore the world and focus strongly on the information that we want. Everything else is, as it were, put on hold.

4 Evaluation

It is tempting to think of attention as a straightforward input-output system. This is the foundation for the single-channel models illustrated in this unit. The question, *'Why do we attend to some things and not others?'* rests on personal, social, environmental, physiological and other factors that are specific to the individual. The question, *'What happens when we do attend?'* goes unanswered. There is no concrete evidence to support the single-channel approach, any more than there is to support other approaches such as Neisser's. Kahnemann tried to explain how tasks can be accomplished seemingly **without** our conscious attention, (e.g. driving a car whilst holding a conversation). Neisser's approach suggests that attention is a developmental process rather than a static structure. Whichever model you feel is most true to life is up to you to decide, but you must know the theories in order to support your view.

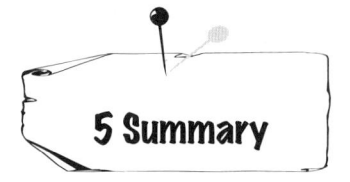

5 Summary

Why do we attend to some things and not others? What happens when we attend?

1 Factors influencing attention
Personal/environmental factors
> Perceptual set, expectation, primacy effects, motivation, emotion, values, level of comfort, distractions

Factors in the object
> Is the data familiar? meaningful? unusual? pleasant?

2 Ways of studying attention
> Shadowing
> Dual-task

3 Theories of attention
> Single channel filters: **Broadbent, Triesman, Deutsch and Deutsch, Norman**
> Limited capacity: **Kahnemann**
> Perceptual cycle: **Neisser**

6 Now ⟹ Over to you...

1 *Fill in the missing words*

(a) Three factors involved in attention are ....; .... and ....

(b) There are two main ways of studying attention. They are s........................ and d........................-t........................

2 *Match the researchers with the model*

(a) Broadbent   (i)   attenuation model
(b) Triesman   (ii)   pertinence model
(c) Deutsch and Deutsch (iii) filter model

3 *Choose the correct name in the sentences*

Kahnemann and Neisser both challenged the single-channel model of attention. Kahnemann/Neisser said that the mind had to decide where best to 'spend' the limited amount of attention it had, while Kahnemann/Neisser said that attention was a skill that could be developed over time.

7 Written exercises

1 What are the factors influencing attention? Give at least one everyday example of how each one works.
2 What ways are there, past and present, of studying attention?
3 Describe each of the single-channel models presented here (and draw the diagram).
4 Describe Kahnemann's ideas about the limited capacity model.
5 How does Neisser's model differ from the single channel models?

8 Topics for discussion

1 What factors do you observe in yourself and others that make you attend to some things and not to others?

2 What factors are there in the things themselves that make you attend to them rather than to others? Give examples of these.

3 How do you think attention works?

4 How can the study of attention help people to communicate a message or sell a product?

5 From your knowledge of the psychology of attention, draw up a list of hints for people hoping to make a good impression on others.

9 Need to know

▸ Can you identify the factors involved that influence attention, and give everyday examples of how they work?
▸ Can you describe different ways of studying attention?
▸ Can you describe how all single channel models operate?

✏ Can you explain the difference between single channel approaches, Kahnemann's approach, and Neisser's approach to the study of attention?

✏ Can you name every psychologist mentioned in this unit and give an account of their work?

10 Suggestions for coursework

1 Design a 'reaction time' experiment looking at differences in speed of reacting to a visual stimulus, an auditory stimulus, or both.

2 Carry out an experiment into the personal factors influencing attention. Give a group a list of words to learn (repeated measures design). Within the lists, include some words that you know are especially meaningful to one or several members of the group. For example, you might know that two people in the group are gardeners. Do they score higher on lists containing the names of flowers than on lists containing the names of household articles?

3 Give two groups of psychology students different lists of words to learn (independent samples design). Give one group a list of words containing some that are meaningful to psychology. Give the other group a list of random words, containing no references to psychology. Compare their scores.

More challenging studies

1 Carry out an experiment to see whether environmental factors have an effect on what is attended to. Ask two groups, Group A and Group B, at different times, to do the same fairly complex learning task. For Group A, keep environmental conditions comfortable. Test Group B in the same conditions, but this time play loud music. (Tell them beforehand that you are going to do this, and remind them of their right to refuse to take part or to withdraw.) How might environmental factors influence attention and therefore learning performance?

Unit Thirteen
Sleep, Dreaming and States of Consciousness

This unit deals with the question

What do we know about states of consciousness?

We are always in a particular state of consciousness, from one extreme of full consciousness when we are highly alert to another extreme when we are deeply unconscious. Our brain/mind is always working, but it works in different ways for different purposes, such as when we are aroused, or when we are dreaming.

The main themes for this topic are:

1 What is the nature of consciousness?
2 What happens when we sleep?
3 What is the purpose of dreaming?
4 Can we control consciousness to help ourselves and others?

1 What is the nature of consciousness?

Consciousness is the name given to the state of our mind/brain when we are awake. **Self-consciousness,** or self-awareness, is the term given to our ability to be aware of our own consciousness. It would appear that this ability is specific to humans, although we do not know about animals since they cannot tell us. Some psychologists say that computers 'think', and are able to 'behave intelligently' (see Unit 11 on Artificial Intelligence), but computers cannot know that they know, whereas humans do. Computers do not have self-consciousness.

Kinds of alertness

Although we may be conscious, we may be alert or aroused to a greater or lesser extent.

Tonic alertness refers to our state of alertness over a long time - e.g. 24 hours, a week, a lifetime. Changes in tonic alertness are slow and often linked to biological and/or maturational factors.

Phasic alertness refers to our state of alertness over short periods - seconds and minutes - and is related to sudden changes in the environment or the self.

Habituation is the name given to the process by which we gradually become used to changes and internalise them as the norm.

Kinds of attention

Focal attention refers to concentrated attention upon a matter in hand - right now you are focally attending to this unit.

Peripheral attention refers to less focused attention - you might be aware of the traffic outside but you are not attending to it particularly.

Sometimes focal attention can get in the way - think what happens when you concentrate too much on striking the right keys when you are typing, for instance, or getting your feet right on the pedals when you are cycling. Sometimes we perform better when we relax and let our bodies take over.

2 What happens when we sleep?

Physiological correlates

Certain changes take place in the body. These match the phases of sleep, so they are called physiological correlates. The EEG of a sleeping person usually shows that the EEG pattern correlates with the four levels of sleep.

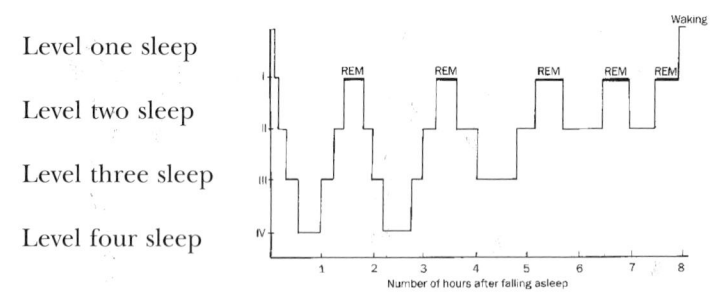

Level one sleep

Level two sleep

Level three sleep

Level four sleep

(adapted from N.Hayes and S.Orrell, 1993)

REM refers to **rapid eye movement**. REM sleep appears to be associated with periods of dreaming. In sleep deprivation studies (e.g. *Dement*) it appears that REM sleep is essential for mental well-being. **NREM (non-REM)** sleep is thought to be essential for tissue repair.

Circadian rhythms (also known as diurnal rhythms)

These are the day-night cycles we tend to live to - our 'body clock' times. Most humans operate over a 24 hour period during which we sleep and we are awake. There are also periods of wakefulness when we are more or less alert. *Aschoff* (1965) and *Miles et al.* (1977) demonstrated that people who are not given external cues about time - e.g. if they are in an environment with no day/night light and no clocks - tend to adjust to a 25 hour cycle.

Implications of these studies

Webb et al. (1971) and *Klein et al.* (1972) studied jet lag effects. Jet lag appears to depend on how well we adjust to new time zones rather than the amount of sleep we have had.

Shiftworkers find that it is less fatiguing if the shifts rotate in such a way that they get later every time, rather than switch entirely to a new pattern.

3 What is the purpose of dreaming?

When do we dream?

Goodenough et al. (1959) and *Webb and Kersey* (1967) discovered that REM sleep is associated with dreaming. Most people appear to dream, though many forget when they wake up. *Dement and Wolpert* studied dreaming as it relates to the external environment such as when the dreamer hears music or is splashed with water. *Hearne* investigated the idea of **lucid dreams** - these studies show that, even though people are asleep, they can still be aware of what they are dreaming about.

Why do we dream? The nature of dreamwork

Theories about why we dream include the following:

Freud believed that the unconscious part of the mind took over from the conscious part during dreaming. Dreaming let the person have experiences that were not available to the conscious mind. Because there was a lot of tension between the conscious mind (ego) and the unconscious mind (id), the material presented in dreams had to be disguised, and so it appeared in symbolic form.

Jung extended Freud's ideas to suggest that dream symbols appeared as **archetypes** - that is, symbols which we all recognise because they are part of our evolution and biological make-up - e.g. water symbolises birth and rebirth; tall towers are phallic symbols.

Crick and Mitchison suggested that dreaming is the way in which we sort the material which we accumulate while we are awake, and get rid of what we do not need. This view of dreamwork suggests that we dream in order to forget what we do not need.

4 Can we control consciousness to help ourselves and others?

It would appear that we can through the practice and use of

> drugs
> biofeedback
> meditation
> hypnosis

Drugs Drugs are usually either stimulants or depressants. They may actively influence our state of consciousness, varying between making us highly alert (e.g. caffeine), and relaxed into unconsciousness (e.g. alcohol).

Biofeedback Biofeedback machines feed back information to the people who are using them about their physiological state - if they are tense or relaxed, for example. This lets the person take steps to control physiological reactions, such as deep slow breathing to slow down the pulse rate.

Meditation This involves positive focusing so that other information is not attended to. This intense focusing seems to help clear the mind/brain, bringing about a state of inner calm.

Hypnosis The idea of suggestibility is at the heart of hypnosis, whether people want to be hypnotised or not. There is no clear evidence to say exactly what happens during hypnosis - whether it is induced by the self or by someone else. Hypnosis appears to be a special state of consciousness which may be used in beneficial ways, such as in pain control.

5 Evaluation

Sleep, dreaming and consciousness are fascinating areas of study, and, probably because they are so interesting and in many ways mysterious, a lot of science fiction and mystique has grown up around them. The authors of this book are not making value judgements here, but we would recommend you to stick to studies involving empirical evidence when you write exercises or examination answers.

A good deal of research is currently going on to investigate different levels of consciousness and their use value. For example, some research is going on into hypnagogia, a state of consciousness between sleeping and waking, when we seem to be highly creative. Another useful area for research is how we can control bodily functions through different states of consciousness, for example through meditation and imaging.

There are a number of interpretations of the function and operations of different levels of consciousness. You need to study the literature and draw your own conclusions, based on your thorough knowledge of what you have studied.

6 Summary

What do we know about states of consciousness?

1 States of consciousness
Consciousness is the state of mind/brain when we are awake. Only humans appear to have self-consciousness.

Kinds of alertness
> Tonic alertness: over a long time
> Phasic alertness: over a short time
> Habituation: getting used to something

Kinds of attention
> focal attention: concentration
> peripheral attention: relaxed awareness

2 What happens when we sleep?
Two kinds of sleep:
> REM sleep - essential for mental repair
> NREM sleep - essential for tissue repair

Circadian rhythms
> Most people work to a 24-hour cycle
> Implications of these studies for helping jetlag effects, and shiftworking arrangements

3 What is the purpose of dreaming?
> When do we dream? - during REM sleep
> Why do we dream? to work with repressed material (***Freud, Jung***);
>> to clear the mind and be refreshed (***Crick and Mitchison***)

4 How can we control consciousness to help ourselves and others?
Through the use of
   drugs, biofeedback, meditation, hypnosis

7 Now ⟹ Over to You ...

1 *Fill in the missing words*

T.................. alertness refers to a person's state of alertness over a long time, while p................ alertness describes the state of alertness over a short time. The name given to the process of getting used to something is h.................. There are two kinds of attention: f....................... attention is concentrating on something, and p.......................... attention is being aware of something but not particularly concentrating on it.

2 *Unscramble the names of these psychologists who have studied the effects of circadian rhythms*

Ffosach, Smile, Bebw, Neilk

3 *Choose the correct version*

REM/NREM refers to rapid eye movement. REM/NREM is essential for mental well-being, while REM/NREM is associated with tissue repair. REM/NREM is associated with dreaming.

4 *Match the psychologist with the theory*

(a) Freud   (i)   said that dreaming was an opportunity to get
                            rid of unwanted material
(b) Jung   (ii) said that dreaming let the person have access to
                            material that had been repressed
(c) Crick and Mitchison (iii) said that dreaming used symbolic archetypes

5 *From the list of words, choose four words that are associated with controlling consciousness*

dreaming, unconsciousness, drugs, biology, biofeedback, symbolic archetypes, meditation, sleep, attention, hypnosis, consciousness, pain control

8 Written exercises

1. Describe different kinds of alertness.
2. When is focal attention a help and when is it a hindrance?
3. Describe the physiological correlates of sleep and the type of sleep.
4. What use can be made of studies of circadian rhythms?
5. Describe the theories of Freud, Jung, and Crick and Mitchison about dreamwork.
6. What is the use of any of the following: drugs, biofeedback, meditation, hypnosis?

9 Topics for discussion

1. Drawing on psychological theories, say why it is important that we get sufficient sleep.

2. What, in your opinion, is the function of dreaming? Draw on your knowledge of psychology to support your answer.

3. Do you think meditation, hypnosis and biofeedback are useful alternatives to conventional medical treatment, or should they not be taken seriously?

10 Need to know

- Can you explain the difference between consciousness and self-consciousness?
- Can you explain the difference between tonic and phasic alertness?
- Can you explain the difference between focal and peripheral attention?
- Can you describe the physiological correlates to the phases of sleep?
- Can you describe the functions of REM and NREM sleep?
- Can you describe the theories of Freud, Jung, and Crick and Mitchison in relation to the nature of dreamwork?
- Can you describe the different ways in which we can control consciousness to help ourselves and others?

11 Suggestions for coursework

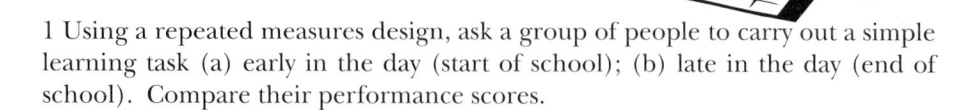

1 Using a repeated measures design, ask a group of people to carry out a simple learning task (a) early in the day (start of school); (b) late in the day (end of school). Compare their performance scores.

2 Using an independent samples design, ask two groups of people to carry out the same learning task, one group early in the day and one group later in the day. Compare their results.

More challenging studies

1 Carry out an experiment into the effects of alertness on performance. Ask a group of people to carry out a simple learning or performance task, such as learning lists of words, or placing pegs in matching holes. Keep a record of their scores on the task at a time when you feel they will be fully alert - at the beginning of the day, or the beginning of the week. Ask them to do the same task, and keep a record of their scores, at other times when you feel they will be less alert or very tired. You will need to control for practice and order effects here. Compare their results.

2 Carry out a survey into what people feel is the function of dreaming. You could extend this by asking people about their own dreaming habits - how often they dream, what kind of dreams they have, and so on.

Unit Fourteen
Intellectual and moral development

This unit deals with the question

How do we develop intellectually and morally?

Intellectual development is about how we come to think and use different kinds of thinking. Moral development is about how we come to tell right from wrong, and apply this in social situations.

The main themes in this topic are

1 How does intellectual development happen?
2 How does moral development happen?
3 What implications are there for individual and social welfare?

1 How does intellectual development happen?

Jean Piaget

Piaget said that babies are born with certain strategies to help them make sense of things. These strategies are schemata. **'Schemata'** is the plural of **'schema'**, a set of ideas or concepts. According to Piaget, development doesn't just happen. It is the result of interaction with the environment, and fitting that experience into existing or new schemata.

Assimilation and accommodation

Piaget thought that development takes place because of two processes:

assimilation   fitting experience into already existing schemata
accommodation   adapting the schemata to accommodate new experience

The processes are in constant interaction with each other.

Stages of development

Piaget believed that all children go through 4 main stages of intellectual development.

Age	Stage	Characteristics
0-2	sensori-motor	egocentric behaviour - thinks 'me'
2-7	pre-operational	egocentric behaviour - fragmented knowledge
7-11	concrete operational	development of conservation and reversal - decentred behaviour
11+	formal operational	development of abstract thinking

Criticisms of Piaget's work

Hughes challenged Piaget's ideas about egocentricity. He showed that children could place dolls in positions so that they could 'see' or 'hide from' each other. This meant that the child had to take the dolls' point of view.

Donaldson argued that children were confused by the task set by Piaget. Children, she said, could make sense of Hughes' task, but not Piaget's.

McGarrigle and Donaldson said that Piaget's experiments on conservation were conducted in a way that did not let the children think for themselves. They replaced the experimenter with a 'naughty teddy'. They felt that children would relate to this situation better.

Jerome Bruner

We have already come across Bruner's work in Unit 6. His ideas run side by side with Piaget's. Bruner says that there are 3 modes of representation, or ways of thinking. These are the **enactive mode,** when we remember things because of the way our body felt at the time; the **iconic mode,** when we turn experience into pictures; and the **symbolic mode,** when we turn the pictures into more abstract symbols such as words. These three ways develop in the child in this order.

2 How does moral development happen?

Jean Piaget's work

Piaget believed that children go through two stages of moral development. These are linked to the stages of cognitive development because Piaget believed that behaving morally depends on thinking. The stages are:

Age	Stage	Characteristics
5-8	autonomous morality	moral realism: moral rules are fixed and imposed by an outside authority
10+	heteronomous morality	morality of co-operation: rules are guidelines to be interpreted

Lawrence Kohlberg's work

Kohlberg based his ideas on and developed them from the ideas of Piaget. He came up with six stages of moral development, consisting of three levels, each with two stages.

Level	Stage	Characteristic
pre-moral (also called pre-conventional)	1	acts morally to avoid punishment
	2	acts morally for approval by others
conventional	3	follows rules because this is the right thing to do
	4	follows rules to keep law and order
post-conventional	5	develops personal moral code
	6	develops 'universal ethic' - is able to reflect on and apply moral reasoning

Kohlberg used a technique of dilemma situations to see what stages of moral development people had reached. He said that not everyone could reach the higher stages.

Sigmund Freud's work
Freud based his ideas about moral development on the balance between the three parts of the personality - the id, ego and super-ego (see also Units 15 and 16). Each part has a different function.

id	pleasure principle	'I want'
ego	reality principle	'I am'
super-ego	moral principle	'I ought'

The super-ego is a kind of parent-figure or conscience, which tells the person what to do. It keeps the id under control, so that the ego can conform to parents' and society's expectations.

3 What implications are there for individual and social welfare?

Piaget's work has been influential in Britain and the West on ideas about the welfare of children and parenting, and have been applied to education, especially pre-school provision. Kohlberg has had a lot of influence, particularly in America. Some areas where their influence is felt are:

Role of family
The family is a major factor in the intellectual and moral development of children. The family atmosphere needs to be happy, supportive and challenging, giving children warmth and emotional security, but also extending them to explore and achieve.

Parenting
There are three main styles of child-rearing (this also applies to styles of leadership):

authoritarian	the parent tells the child what to do
democratic	the parent discusses with the child and they work out decisions together
laissez-faire (permissive)	the parent lets the child do what s/he wants

A democratic style seems to most useful in encouraging children to think for themselves while being sensitive to the needs of others.

Child minding
There is some debate about whether children find it difficult to relate to their parents as well as child minders. Bowlby would have something to say about this! (Unit 15)

Pre-school provision
The emphasis today in pre-school provision is to provide a warm and secure environment in which children may explore and discover their world.

Play
Play is recognised as a vital aspect in development. It helps

physical development	muscle co-ordination, development of fine and gross motor skills
social development	children learn to adapt to and get on with each other
emotional development	children may develop a feeling of self-worth
intellectual development	children can explore the way they think in a supportive, protective but challenging environment
moral development	children can explore concepts of right and wrong through being together

4 Evaluation

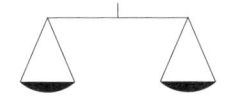

There is criticism of Piaget's work, more about the way he carried out his investigations than his findings and ideas. However, he has had a lot of influence on the way that people think about intellectual and moral development, and the way that development can be encouraged. Kohlberg also is a major influence, particularly in the USA. You should be aware of the basic ideas in their approaches and see how they relate to parenting and child-rearing skills, and the implications they have for education, particularly pre-school provision, and the training of carers and educators.

5 Summary

How do we develop intellectually and morally?

1 How does intellectual development happen?

Piaget says that the two processes of assimilation and accommodation help us to make sense of the world. There are four stages of development:
- sensori-motor
- pre-operational
- concrete operational
- formal operational

Criticisms of Piaget's work (***Hughes, Donaldson, McGarrigle***) challenge the method more than the findings.

Bruner says there are three ways of making sense: the enactive mode, the iconic mode, and the symbolic mode.

2 How does moral development happen?

Piaget believes there are two stages of moral development:
- autonomous morality
- heteronomous morality

Kohlberg believes there are three main levels of moral development, which each operates at two stages.
- pre-moral (or pre-conventional)
- conventional
- post-conventional

Not everyone reaches all the stages, so not everyone is fully developed morally.

Freud believes that moral behaviour is the result of the super-ego supervising the ego and keeping the id in control.

3 Implications for individual and social welfare

The role of the family is very important.
Parents need to develop good parenting skills.
Child minding is a question that is frequently debated.
Pre-school provision stresses the need for a warm, supporting and challenging environment for the child to explore and discover.
Play is an essential part of children's physical, social, emotional, intellectual and moral development.

6 Now Over to you...

1 *Fill in the missing words*

(a) Piaget believed that intellectual development takes place because of the two processes of as........................... and ac...............................

(b) Bruner believed that we use three ways of thinking, or modes of representation. These are the e.......................... mode, the ic...................... mode and the sym........................ mode. The order in which they develop in humans is this: (1) .... (2) .... (3) ....

2 *Fill in the missing words*

These areas are important in child-rearing: role of the family, pa........................, pre-s.............. p............................ Play is particularly important because it helps development in these areas: phy......................., so......................., em......................., intel........................., mor................

3 *In the charts below, fill in the missing words from the lists provided.*

Piaget's stages of development
egocentric behaviour, pre-operational, formal operational

Age	Stage	Characteristic
1-2	sensori-motor	
2-7		egocentric behaviour - fragmented knowledge
7-11	concrete operational	development of conservation and reversal - decentred behaviour
11+		development of abstract thinking

Piaget's stages of moral development

Autonomous morality; morality of co-operation; rules are guidelines to be interpreted.

Age	Stage	Characteristic
5-8		moral realism: fixed and imposed by outside authority
10+	heterenomous morality	

Kohlberg's stages of moral development

Acts morally for approval by others, follows rules because this is the right thing to do, post conventional, develops 'universal ethic'- is able to reflect on and apply moral reasoning.

Level	Stage	Characteristic
pre-moral	1	acts morally to avoid punishment
	2	
conventional	3	
	4	follows rules to keep law and order
	5	develops personal moral code
	6	

Freud's model of moral development

Want, reality principle, super-ego, 'I ought',

id	pleasure principle	'I '
ego		'I am'
	moral principle	

7 Written exercises

1 Describe the processes of assimilation and accommodation.
2 Describe Piaget's stages for intellectual development.
3 Outline any two criticisms of Piaget's work.
4 What were Bruner's three modes of representation?
5 Describe how moral development happens, according to Piaget and Kohlberg. Show the differences between the two.
6 How did Kohlberg show that moral development had taken place?
7 Describe Freud's model of moral development.
8 Describe any three ways in which children's development can be encouraged.

8 Topics for discussion

1 Do you think it is possible to trace the development of intellectual and moral development in children in the ways that Piaget and Kohlberg are suggesting?

2 If you were a headteacher or a governor of a nursery school, how would you arrange the school to take account of the ideas of Piaget?

3 Is play as important for adolescents and adults as it is for children?

4 Do you agree with Kohlberg that some people do not seem to reach full moral development?

9 Need to know

▷ Can you explain the concepts of assimilation and accommodation?

▷ Can you describe Piaget's stages of intellectual and moral development?

▷ Can you explain Bruner's ideas about intellectual development?

▷ Can you describe Freud's and Kohlberg's models of moral development?

▷ Can you explain the difference between the models of moral development of Piaget, Kohlberg and Freud? Can you give a critical evaluation of each one?

▷ Can you talk about the ways in which these ideas can be applied to the care of young children and parenting skills?

▷ Can you name all the psychologists mentioned in this unit, and describe their work?

10 Suggestions for coursework

1 Try to replicate the conservation experiments of Piaget and/or Hughes.

2 Conduct an observational study of children at play to test the hypothesis that 'boys are more aggressive than girls'. Use categories of behaviour that describe aggression and non-aggression.

More challenging studies

1 Try to replicate the conservation experiments of Piaget and Hughes. Using Hughes' criticism of Piaget's methods, draw some conclusions about the ability of children to use decentred styles of thinking.

2 Conduct an extended case study to show how a child moves from egocentric to decentred thinking. (This would not be suitable for GCSE work, as it would have to be done over a period of time.)

3 Conduct a survey, using attitude scales and questionnaires, about the usefulness of Kohlberg's approach to measuring moral development. Give your participants Kohlberg's famous example: *The only thing that could save a man's dying wife was a very expensive drug which a chemist had taken years to develop. The man could not afford the drug so he asked the chemist to give him some. The chemist refused, so the man stole it. Was he right?* Give your participants some answers based on Kohlberg's levels of moral development, and ask them if they think answers like these really can measure moral development.

4 Conduct an observational study of children at play, to see whether they show egocentric or decentred behaviour. Use categories of behaviour that would be representative of egocentric and decentred behaviour. Remember to get permission to observe the children in this way.

Unit Fifteen
Attachment and separation

This unit deals with the questions

What is the nature of parent-child interaction?
What significance has attachment for personal development and socialisation?

It is often thought that good parent-child interactions are essential for the successful socialisation of the child, but there is contradictory evidence here. Is lack of attachment the only reason for lack of socialisation? What do we understand by successful socialisation?

The main points here are:

1 How do children develop attachments to other people?
2 What theories of attachment are there?
3 What significance have these studies for the care of young children and parenting skills?

1 How do children develop attachments to other people?

Parent-child interaction

Socialisation is the process through which a child learns to become a member of society and internalises accepted social norms. Some theories stress the role of parents in socialisation. The process of attachment appears to go on from birth, but becomes significant at about 7 months. This attachment bond is usually the child's first step to socialisation.

Sociability of the child

Humans seem to have a strong inclination towards sociability. Newborn infants (neonates) will react and smile at all kinds of familiar stimuli, including people and manufactured faces (see the work of Fantz, Unit 3). *Ahrens* (1954) also demonstrated the infant's tendency to smile at human faces.

Attachment and interaction

Attachment bonds seem to develop more quickly if parents and infants are able to interact. *Stern* (1977) showed how parents behaved to communicate with their infants, and meet their needs, particularly in the development of 'body talk'. *Shaffer* investigated how parents and infants take turns in 'dialogue' - what he calls 'interlocution'. **Crying** is a powerful signal to parents, and **eye contact** is probably the most important way of communicating (see particularly *Schaffer* and *Emerson*, who investigated bonding between infants and their caretakers; also *Bennett*, who found that eye contact could be the most significant factor; *Fraiberg*, who noted that mothers of blind babies can feel rejected when eye contact is not established, and therefore need to develop coping strategies for this event; and *Klaus*, who also investigated how mothers saw their children as real people through the establishment of eye contact).

Fear of strangers

Fear of strangers, a concept related to the work of *Mary Ainsworth*, develops over the first few months of baby's life. This seems to be part of the process by which infants learn to discriminate between the preferred adult and others.

Preferred adult

The **preferred adult** is usually the person who interacts most in accordance with baby's liking. This is usually the mother, though not necessarily so. Neither is it always the 'caregiver' - i.e. the person who looks after the child.

Harlow's work

Harlow's work with rhesus monkeys indicated that infant monkeys needed comfort and security as a main priority. If infants were separated from their parents at birth, they missed a critical period for forming an attachment, which had serious implications for socialisation in later life. Although it is not a good idea to draw too close a comparison between the reactions of monkeys and the reactions of children, some psychologists draw on Harlow's findings to support their theories of attachment and socialisation.

Note: Imprinting and bonding can both be regarded as forms of attachment at GCSE level. Imprinting is the name given to the rapid learning that happens in lower-order animals; bonding is the process of forming a bond between human infants and adults.

2 Theories of attachment

The theorists whose work you need to know for this course are *Mary Ainsworth, Sigmund Freud, John Bowlby, Michael Rutter and Anna Freud.*

1 Mary Ainsworth

Mary Ainsworth studied attachment between parents and infants through the **'strange situation'**, a procedure of 8 fixed actions involving parents and a stranger entering and leaving a room where an infant is. She categorised 3 kinds of attachment based on observation of how the infants reacted to the situation:

secure attachment, where the child is reasonably confident, well adjusted and self-aware;
insecure attachment, where the child tends to cling to its parents and is reluctant to venture out on its own;
unattached, where the child seems indifferent to whether the parent is there or not.

Factors contributing to which kind of attachment develops are:

(a) **temperament of the child**, whether friendly and good natured, or bad-tempered;
(b) **behaviour of parents towards the child,** whether sympathetic to the child and responding to its needs, or expecting the child to adapt to them.

The more parents accept the child on its own terms, the more securely attached it appears to be. (This says nothing about how the parents might feel!)

2 Sigmund Freud

Freud's work is known as the **psychoanalytical approach**, and is discussed also in the next Unit on Gender and Socialisation. Freud believed that attachment happened during the first five years of life, and was related to the different **psychosexual stages** that the child went through. The important stages were the oral stage, the anal stage, and the phallic stage (at about 4/5 years old). Freud's emphasis was on boys (females were not entirely recognised in those days), and his main idea about attachment was how a boy developed a desire for a sexual relationship with his mother, and began to see his father as a rival.

However, the boy would decide to '**identify with the aggressor**' - that is, joined sides with the father for fear that father might castrate him (this was based on the story of King Oedipus). During the phallic stage, the boy learned to identify with his father, through **resolution of the Oedipus complex.** Other Freudian theorists applied the same idea to girls, saying that girls developed penis envy, because they believed themselves to be already castrated. This leads a girl to seek a strong love attachment with her father, and she finally identifies with her mother in order to become like her - the **resolution of the Electra complex.**

Freud thought that the personality began developing in childhood through interaction with the parents: for Freud, the personality was the **id**, the **ego** and the **superego**. A balance between these three parts meant that the personality as a whole was balanced, and the person had no mental and emotional problems. If the three parts were out of balance, then the person experienced problems. The superego was a kind of conscience, and took the role of authoritarian father. The adult personality would depend on how well the child and parent had developed an attachment. If the superego (father-figure) was too well developed, the person would feel oppressed.

Freud's psychoanalytical approach to childhood attachment must be clearly distinguished from **Social Learning Theory,** which is associated with the work of *Bandura*, and is discussed in more detail in Unit 16. Social Learning Theory says that children learn their behaviour from observing adults and copying them. Attachments would form through children taking on the same behaviours as the adults with whom they were interacting.

3 John Bowlby

Bowlby was influenced by Harlow's work, which drew on the idea of a **critical period** for attachment. He thought that unless a firm attachment was made with its mother during the first 5 years of a child's life, the child would develop **affectionless psychopathy** - that is, not be able to feel any kind of warmth for anyone else, or be concerned with their welfare. Any separation from the mother - **maternal deprivation** - could result in physical and psychological problems, and delinquency in adolescence. Having studied 44 delinquent adolescents, 17 of whom had experienced separation from their mothers before the age of 5, Bowlby concluded that maternal deprivation caused delinquency. Bowlby's theory is also called **monotropy theory** - that is, the child relates only to its mother.

4 Michael Rutter

Rutter disagreed with Bowlby's views. He studied adolescent boys to see if there was a relationship between delinquent or antisocial behaviour and early separation due to hospitalisation and also due to family problems. He found that when children returned to a stable environment after hospitalisation or other institutionalisation, they would settle down and in fact be less inclined to antisocial behaviour. Rutter felt that family arguments and an unsettled environment were causes of anti-social behaviour in young people.

Rutter argued that Bowlby was mistaken in drawing on and relating his work with children to the work of Harlow with monkeys because of these factors:

Harlow	**Bowlby**
- conducted privation studies (lack of mother)	- conducted deprivation studies (losing mother)
- used an experimental method	- used an observational method
- worked with monkeys	- worked with children

5 Anna Freud

Anna Freud conducted case studies of a group of 6 orphaned children from a concentration camp. She discovered that, although the children experienced difficulties in relating to adults, they were firmly committed to each other. They regarded their peers as the central figures of attachment, rather than parents. This work suggests, like Rutter's, that bonding with the mother is not always necessary for successful attachment and socialisation.

3 The significance of studies of attachment for the care of young children and parenting skills

Practical applications of the work outlined with regard to the care of young children include:

❏ Children need at least one firm, caring relationship from an early age; this relationship would be with the main caregiver who is usually, but not always, the child's preferred adult; this relationship needs to last throughout the first years of the child's life.
❏ Children need a secure environment, in which they feel they have a clear identity and a role to play.
❏ They need good role models whose behaviour they will imitate.
❏ They need praise and warmth.
❏ They need positive affirmation that they are loved and valued.
❏ Caregivers need to be consistent in their attitudes towards, and dealings with, children - they must not be moody, or in any way 'blow hot and cold'.
❏ Caregivers need to cater for the child's wants and needs on a sensible basis.
❏ The environment should be rich in stimuli and resources to encourage exploration, discovery and creativity.
❏ Caregivers and children need to spend time together in play and exploration.
❏ Caregivers need to encourage play and exploration amongst children, while keeping an eye on appropriate behaviour.

4 Evaluation

It is very tempting to draw quick conclusions about what is needed to bring about the socialisation of young children. Many ideas have been challenged and exploded. Mothers are not necessarily the main caregivers, though this is still a commonly held opinion. Indeed, neither parent may be the main caregiver or preferred adult. It is also very tempting to say that anti-social behaviour can be put down to poor parenting, though this is often the case. Nor can it be put down to single-parenting. There is no evidence that anti-social behaviour is the result of single parenting.

Bowlby's work has been critiqued by a number of psychologists, including Rutter, because
(a) his sample group was very small;
(b) not everyone who suffered maternal deprivation turned out to be a delinquent, and not everyone who was a delinquent suffered maternal deprivation.

Attachment is of course a big factor in the happiness of children, but the attachment may come from a variety of sources. Preferred adult, peers, toys, etc. can all provide a source of emotional stability. Provided they develop enough emotional stability, children should have a positive experience of childhood and grow into responsible and well-adjusted adults.

5 Summary

What is the nature of parent-child interaction?
What significance has attachment for personal development and socialisation?

1 How do children develop attachments?

Factors involved include
     parent-child attachment
     sociability of the child
     attachment and interaction
     fear of strangers
     preferred adult
Harlow's work is important for giving insights into the nature of attachment.

2 What theories of attachment are there?

Attachment behaviour
    Ainsworth   secure attachment
                         insecure attachment
                         unattached

Psychoanalytical theories
    Freud (identification with the aggressor through resolution of the Oedipus complex)

Deprivation studies
    Bowlby (affectionless psychopathy; monotropy theory; maternal deprivation)
    Rutter (adolescent delinquent boys)

Privation studies
    (*Harlow*: see section above: worked with rhesus monkeys)
    Anna Freud (group of orphaned children)

3 Implications for the care of young children

There are many factors involved in bringing about socialisation in young children. The main factors are to do with providing a good degree of emotional stability through interpersonal relationships. Children need a warm, caring environment in which to develop, with clear role models and signposts about acceptable behaviour.

6 Now ⇒ over to you...

1 *Complete the following sentences*

(a) Socialisation is..
....
(b) Attachment bonds develop more rapidly if parents and children
....
....
(c) The preferred adult is the person who ....
....
(d) Fear of strangers is ....
....

2 *Fill in the missing names*

(a) .... investigated 'the strange situation'.
(b) .... believed that children form attachments with parents through identification.
(c) .... believed that maternal deprivation led to juvenile delinquency.
(d) .... believed that anti-social behaviour was caused more by family arguments than by maternal deprivation.
(e) ....investigated attachments between people other than between children and parents.

3 *From the list given, choose three factors that are important in the care of young children*

maternal deprivation, warmth in relationships, sweets, observations, stimulating environment, family studies, the Oedipus complex, play, television, psychology

7 Written exercises

1 What factors need to be taken into consideration when we are studying how attachments between children and adults develop?
2 Describe the work of Harlow, Ainsworth, Freud, Bowlby, Rutter and Anna Freud.
3 Show how there are major differences between the work of any two of the psychologists mentioned in (2).
4 From the work that you have studied in this unit, what might the practical implications be for (a) the care of young children; (b) parenting skills?

8 Topics for discussion

1 From your knowledge of the psychology of attachment and separation, what recommendations would you make for the social arrangements of nursery and primary schools?

2 How can hospitals and other institutions try to reduce distress to children while they are away from home?

3 What advice would you give to parents of an only child to help the child's socialisation?

9 Need to know

▸ Can you say what main factors encourage children to develop attachments?

▸ Can you describe the work of Mary Ainsworth, Sigmund Freud, John Bowlby, Michael Rutter, Anna Freud?

▸ Can you critically evaluate their theories?

▸ Can you say what implications studies of attachment have for the care of young children and parenting skills?

10 Suggestions for coursework

1 Carry out a survey into public opinion about the causes of anti-social behaviour. In particular, try to find out whether people feel that this behaviour is the result of maternal deprivation, and relate your findings to the work of Bowlby and Rutter.

2 Carry out an observational study into the kinds of behaviour that you feel are necessary for good parenting or the care of young children. You may be able to get permission to go to nursery schools or playgroups. Otherwise, watch adults with children in public places, and see the way they behave. You will need to devise behaviour categories for this.

More challenging studies

1 Carry out a survey into the kinds of provision made in your area for the welfare of young children. Relate this to the work of the psychologists mentioned in this unit. You might, for example, approach your local hospital, and find out what arrangements there are for parents to visit children; or you might contact the Education Department or Social Services to enquire about amenities such as playgroup or nursery provision for the under-fives.

2 Conduct a survey into the causes of anti-social behaviour such as football hooliganism or street violence. Relate this particularly to single parenting. Is there any relationship?

Unit Sixteen
Gender and socialisation

This unit deals with the questions

Is gender a significant factor in socialisation?
Why do children often act according to the way society sees gender roles?

Gender identity is very important in the socialisation of boys and girls and the development of their social role. Some people think that boys and girls are born with certain innate tendencies to adopt so-called 'masculine' and 'feminine' roles, while others believe that social role is entirely learned.

The main themes in this topic are:

1 The biological influence on sexual development; the biological differences between males and females; the influences of hormones on sexual development.
2 Approaches to sex identity and socialisation, including the psychoanalytical approach and the social learning approach.
3 A critical evaluation of these approaches and an evaluation of the evidence provided by each approach.

1 Biological factors

Some definitions

Sex refers to biological differences between males and females.
Gender refers to perceived social differences between males and females.
Sexuality refers to aspects of behaviour that are sexual in nature.

Biological differences between males and females fall into three main categories

(a) **Chromosomal sex:** all human beings have 23 pairs of chromosomes - 46 altogether. Every human being has a special pair of chromosomes relating to sex - in females this pair of chromosomes is XX; in males it is XY.

(b) **Gonadal sex:** this refers to the organs of reproduction - testes in males and ovaries in females.

(c) **Hormonal sex**: males produce hormones called androgens, the most important being testosterone, released by the testes. Females produce oestrogen and progesterone, released by the ovaries. Both males and females produce all hormones, but males produce more male hormones, and females produce more female hormones.

It has been demonstrated in some animals that sex-role behaviour can be induced by hormones. Male rats can 'mother' young, for example, having been injected with an appropriate hormone. It is unlikely that purely biological influences can produce sex-role behaviour in humans, although this is a view taken by the biological approach (see below).

2 Approaches to sex identity and socialisation

1 The biological approach

This view suggests that biological factors are the reason for gender role differences in males and females. There are some significant differences, apart from biological ones. For example, studies indicate that females tend to live longer than males, have higher tolerance rates to many conditions, are more adaptable and docile. These biological differences suggest that females might be more suited to caring roles, while males might be more suited to active, demanding roles in society.

2 The biosocial approach

This theory says that biological differences influence the expectations of parents and other adults, and also influence the way that boys and girls are treated. *Money and Ehrhardt* studied hermaphrodites and pseudo-hermaphrodites (people with the physical attributes of both sexes) and found that there was a lot of flexibility in the first 2 or 3 years of life as regards children's own perception of their sex-role. After about the age of 3, children settle into perceiving themselves as a particular gender, probably because of increasing awareness of social influences and expectations.

3 Freud's psychoanalytical approach

Freud believed that the traditional roles of strong, aggressive father and nurturant mother were essential for the mental and physical well-being of the child. In terms of Freud's theory of psychosexual development, the child has to resolve the Oedipus complex at about 5 years of age. This is when the boy develops a passionate love for the mother, sees father as a potential rival, but identifies with the aggressor through fear of castration. In this way, the boy develops a male role, so that he and his father are seen as a team. The same situation happens for girls through resolution of the Electra complex. Freud and his followers believed that if children did not have these traditional sex role models, they would grow up as homosexual.

4 The social learning approach

This view says that children learn their gender roles through observation and imitation (***Bandura et al.***). They learn how to behave from watching adults, and their own gender-linked behaviour is then reinforced. ***Smith and Lloyd,*** and ***Sears et al.***, found that parents encouraged gender-role behaviour by, for example, approving rough and tumble play in boys but not in girls, choice of toys, and so on. Such attitudes are strongly reinforced throughout the growing child's life through messages from TV and other media, and through their own developing gender-role attitudes.

5 Androgyny

In 1975, Sandra Bem studied the similarities, rather than differences, between males and females, arguing that males and females possessed both 'masculine' and 'feminine' characteristics. This raises the question of whether 'masculine' or 'feminine' characteristics are biologically or socially determined in the first place. Bem argued that this was a more healthy foundation for children's psychological development.

3 Evaluation

It seems that biological differences do not account for the socialisation process that boys and girls go through. Empirical evidence for this can also be found in cross-cultural studies; in some cultures, females are seen as dominant while the men develop nurturing, compliant roles. Also, gender roles change within the same culture over time; in the 1850s, more women went down the mines in Britain than men.

There is strong evidence to suggest that gender role is learned from society, although this may itself be a result of genetic factors, as the biosocial approach suggests.

Much of Freud's psychoanalytical approach would today seem to be mistaken. For example, **Golombok et al.** (1983) studied children brought up in lesbian and single-parent families. They compared them with children from more traditional heterosexual households, and found that the children had no gender role or sex role confusion.

Very promising future research could be in the study of androgyny, where human characteristics are thought to be distributed across the population. It is open to question whether such characteristics are shown to be 'male' or 'female' (see, for example, *Gilligan et al., Women's Ways of Knowing*). This kind of research may well change thinking about gender role, seeing it not so much as to do with sex-identity (psychological orientation) as with learned gender role (sociological orientation).

4 Summary

Is gender a significant factor in socialisation? Why do children often act according to the way society sees gender roles?

1 Biological factors

Chromosomal sex: XX and XY
Gonadal sex: testes/ovaries
Hormonal sex: androgens (testosterone) in males; oestrogen and progesterone in females.

2 Approaches

Biological approach: genetic factors determine sex identity and gender role.
Biosocial approach: genetic factors and social interaction determine gender role.
Psychoanalytical approach: conflict and resolution of Oedipus and Electra conflict influences sex and gender role.
Social learning approach: gender role is learned and internalised through observation and imitation.
Androgyny: males and females have 'masculine' and 'feminine' characteristics.

3 Evaluations

Biological approach: Extreme view - suggests that gender role is determined by genetic inheritance. Possibly so in animal experiments testing hormone-induced behaviour.

Biosocial approach: Balanced view - suggests interaction of genetic and social factors. Still plays down emphasis on learned behaviour in social gender role.

Psychoanalytical approach: Extreme view suggesting that sexual identity occurs during the phallic stage at 3-5 years.

Social learning approach: balanced view suggesting social foundation of gender-related behaviour, learned through imitation.

Androgyny: balanced view suggesting that psychology ought to investigate more the similarities between males and females rather than the differences.

5 Now ⇒ over to you ....

1 *Fill in the missing words*

(a) .... refers to biological differences between males and females.
(b) .... refers to perceived social differences between males and females.
(c) .... refers to aspects of behaviour that are sexual in nature.

2 *Match the approach with the description*

(a) The biological approach	(i)	suggests interaction of genetic and social factors
(b) The biosocial approach	(ii)	suggests that males and females share common characteristics
(c) The psychoanalytical approach	(iii)	suggests that gender role is determined through genetic inheritance
(d) The social learning approach	(iv)	suggests that sex identity is fixed during the phallic stage
(e) The androgyny approach	(v)	suggests that gender role behaviour is learned through imitation

3 *Unscramble the names of some psychologists who study gender and socialisation*

Aburand, Dyoll, Meb, Kobmolog, Druef

4 *Which one of these statements does not refer to studies on gender and socialisation?*

(a) The biosocial approach and the psychoanalytical approach present different kinds of evidence in the study of gender and socialisation.
(b) The social learning approach emphasises the role that adults play in teaching children how to behave correctly.
(c) Freud's psychoanalytical approach is not to be confused with the social learning approach.
(d) According to some psychologists, maternal deprivation is the cause of juvenile delinquency.
(e) The biological approach says that biological factors decide gender role.

6 Written exercises

1 Explain the differences between these terms: sex identity, gender role, sexuality.
2 Outline the three main biological factors in determining sex identity.
3 Describe each of the following:

   the biological approach
   the biosocial approach
   the psychoanalytical approach
   the social learning approach
   the androgyny approach

4 Outline the strengths and limitations in each of the approaches mentioned at (3).

5 Give a critical evaluation of the psychoanalytical and social learning approaches, and an evaluation of the implications of each approach.

7 Topics for discussion

1 What, in your opinion, is the major influence in the development of gender role?
2 To what extent do the media communicate and reinforce messages to do with gender role?
3 How can thinking about gender roles be modified?

8 Need to know

- Can you explain when the terms 'sex', 'gender' and 'sexuality' are used?
- Can you explain the terms 'chromosomal sex', 'gonadal sex', 'hormonal sex'?
- Can you describe clearly the following approaches and the differences between them?
    - the biological approach
    - the biosocial approach
    - the psychoanalytical approach
    - the social learning approach
    - the androgyny approach
- Can you give a critical evaluation of each one?

9 Suggestions for coursework

1 Carry out an observational study on how gender roles are reinforced, or not, through the media, by watching TV programmes or advertisements. Note which roles are taken by females and males - for example, who does the washing in washing powder advertisements, and who does the voice-overs? Do 'role-reversal' situations actually reverse or reinforce stereotypical roles?

2 Carry out a survey into gender role differences in order to investigate public opinion on women and male roles (a) at work; (b) in the home and family.

More challenging studies

1 Conduct an investigation to see whether certain professions reinforce gender role stereotypes. Carry out a survey of a group of police officers, or nurses, or teachers, and see whether stereotyping is more evident within one profession than another.

2 You could extend this study to investigate gender role stereotyping within certain organisations, such as in hospitals, schools and colleges, nursery schools, businesses. Although equality of opportunity is a legal requirement in the United Kingdom, is it always carried out in practice?

3 Carry out an observational study to see how parents might or might not reinforce traditional roles by watching parents interacting with children in a playgroup, or in a public place, or in an educational setting. Remember to obtain the necessary permissions.

Unit Seventeen
Social Perception

This unit deals with the questions

How do we perceive other people? How do other people perceive us?

Social perception is about forming impressions of other people. Very often we don't have a lot of information to go on, so we have to make quick decisions. There seem to be certain psychological principles to help us make those decisions.

> **The things that help us make those decisions are the main themes of this topic:**
>
> 1 What kind of things do we believe about other people (personality theories)?
> 2 How important are first impressions (primacy and recency effects)?
> 3 How do we explain other people's actions (attribution theory)?

1 Implicit personality theories

These are the theories we have (things we believe) about other people. We tend to form impressions about people in the light of our previous experience of other people who looked or acted like them. We often group characteristics together to form theories about the whole person - we would group together characteristics such as 'generous', 'kind', and 'sense of humour'; and 'miserable', 'mean', 'unsociable'.

Asch (1946) found that we use the two main labels of 'warm' and 'cold' as **central character traits**. Other characteristics appeared to be secondary. This is also a good example of the **halo effect,** when we attribute other positive qualities to a person on the basis of a very limited but strong piece of information.

Harold Kelley (1950) found that if he described a visiting lecturer to a group of students using those central traits, the students would actually be biased for or against the visitor.

2 Primacy and recency effects

Asch also researched the way our perceptions are influenced by the order in which we receive information. He gave one group (A) of people this list of words describing someone: *intelligent, industrious, impulsive, critical, stubborn, envious.* Another group (B) was given the list: *critical, stubborn, envious, intelligent, industrious, impulsive.* Group A saw the person in a favourable light; Group B saw the person in a negative light. The effects of the order in which things are presented to us are called **primacy and recency effects.**

Luchins also investigated primacy and recency effects. He gave participants a story about 'Jim', containing two paragraphs. One paragraph showed Jim as friendly and outgoing; the other paragraph described him as introverted. Some participants were given the 'outgoing' paragraph first, and the others were given the 'introverted' paragraph first. The participants were then asked to describe Jim's personality. Luchins found that all participants judged Jim in terms of the first paragraph they had read.

It seems that first impressions have the strongest impact. This has implications for job interviews and so on. This is known as the **primacy effect**.

However, when the first impression fades over time, and new information is introduced, the new information will be the most strongly perceived. This is known as the recency effect. For example, imagine that you did not particularly like someone the first time you met them. However, when you met them again a few months later, they acted differently and you found yourself liking them. This second, more recent, impression will probably be the one you remember.

3 Attribution theory

This is one way that we judge other people's behaviour. We explain their actions in terms of whether we think the actions were because of the person's character (**dispositional attribution**) or because of the situation (**situational attribution**). We are more likely to help a person who has slipped up if we see a banana skin lying nearby (situational attribution) than if the person is smelling of drink (dispositional attribution).

Kelley (1967) thinks that the information that lets us make judgements about the person's actions (whether they are dispositional or situational attributes) falls into three categories:

(a) **Has the behaviour high consensus** - i.e. are lots of other people doing the same thing?
(b) **Is the behaviour consistent** - does the person always act like this?
(c) **Is the behaviour distinctive** - does the person act like this only in certain situations?

Attributional bias

We tend to judge other people's behaviour in terms of dispositional attribution - *'He dropped the plate because he is clumsy'* - and our own in term of situational attribution - *'I dropped the plate because it was slippery.'* This bias also leads to the **fundamental attribution error.** This is when we think that others are entirely responsible for their own behaviour - *'She receives benefit because she can't be bothered to find a job'*, rather than, *'She receives benefit because there are no jobs available'*; or, *'He doesn't understand because he is not intelligent'*, rather than, *'He doesn't understand because I am not explaining this clearly.'*

4 Evaluation

Social perception as a topic of study is part of the wider field of perception in general. Psychologists working in social perception tend to come to their theories through an 'other-perspective', that is, approaching the study from the point of view of how one individual reacts to another. They tend not to see their work in terms of how the individual is perceiving reality in general. This will clearly bias the individual's perception of others. Although you are studying social perception as an self-contained unit, it is important for you to appreciate how all areas of psychological enquiry relate to each other.

Social perception studies suggest general principles about how people perceive each other, but, when we relate these principles to everyday life, it is important to remember the situational and personal factors that affect individuals as well.

5 Summary

How do we see other people? How do other people see us?

1 Implicit theories
The central characteristic traits which are most important are 'warm', 'cold' (***Asch*** and ***Kelley***)

2 Primacy and recency effects

First impressions are the strongest. If they fade over time, more recent impressions become strongest (**Asch** and **Luchins**).

3 Attribution theory

There are two kinds of attribution:
Dispositional attribution (It's the person's nature/fault)
Situational attribution (It's the situation's nature/fault)
Kelley asked three questions about behaviour:
Has it high consensus?
Is it consistent?
Is it distinctive?

The answers to these questions help us to decide whether the behaviour can be blamed on the person (dispositional attribution) or on the situation (situational attribution).

4 Attributional bias leading to the fundamental attribution error

We are quick to judge other people but not so quick to judge ourselves. We usually see other people's actions in terms of dispositional bias, and our own in terms of situational bias.

6 Now ➡ Over to you...

1 *Fill in the missing words*

The two central characteristic traits that were identified by A.................... were 'w......................' and 'c............................'.

2 When we form an impression about someone based on the first piece of information we have, this is known as the ....
When we form an impression about someone based on the latest information that we have, this is known as the ....

3 *Choose the correct words*

Dispositional attribution refers to factors ***in the person/in the situation*** and situational attribution refers to factors ***in the person/in the situation.***

4 *Which of these situations would you put down to (a) dispositional attribution; (b) situational attribution?*

(a) The plate broke while I was drying it because it was already cracked.
(b) He broke the plate because he is clumsy.
(c) He can't do the work because he has not done the necessary preparation.
(d) I can't do the work because I have left my spectacles at home.

5 *Fill in the missing words*
Question 4 tells us that we often make judgements about other people in terms of d.............................. a.............................., but we judge ourselves in terms of s......................... a............................. This is known as a............................. b...................... .

6 When we say that everything is a person's own fault, we are making the f.............................. a.................................... e........................

7 Written exercises

1 Why is it important to choose our words carefully when we are describing a person to someone else?
2 Why is it important to create a good first impression? If we fail to make a good impression the first time, what can we do to put the situation right?
3 What is the difference between dispositional attribution and situational attribution?
4 What is the fundamental attribution error? Give two examples of this in everyday life.

8 Topics for discussion

1) You are writing a handbook for trainee salespersons. What advice, based on your knowledge of psychology, would you give to help them make a good impression?
2) Drawing on the theories outlined in this unit, explain how we make judgements about other people's behaviour and our own.

9 Need to know

▭ Can you say what implicit personality theories are?

▭ Can you name the central character traits?

▭ Can you describe primacy and recency effects and how they work?

▭ Can you explain what attribution theory is and how it works?

▭ Can you explain the difference between dispositional attribution and situational attribution?

▭ Can you explain what the fundamental attribution error is?

▭ Can you name all the psychologists mentioned in this unit, and describe their work?

10 Suggestions for coursework

1 Carry out an experiment into primacy and recency effects by replicating the work of Luchins. Here is a variation on the theme which you might like to try out. Organise two groups of participants. You will be able to work with both groups at the same time if you wish. Give Group A a list of words describing someone, with positive attributes first in the list. Give Group B a list of words describing someone, with negative attributes first on the list. When the groups have studied the lists, remove the lists and administer a short questionnaire to find out if the two groups see the person described in a favourable or unfavourable light.

2 Carry out a survey into situational and dispositional attribution by asking people how they would react in particular situations: for example, *'Would you help someone who had fallen off a bike accidentally?'* and *'Would you help someone who had fallen off a bike they had stolen?'*

More challenging studies

1 Conduct an investigation into dispositional and attributional disposition. Show people a series of pictures of people in a difficult situation, such as having fallen over. Include a written explanation about the people in the pictures, either putting their difficulty down to some aspect of their personality or to some aspect of the situation. Check how people come to their judgements.

2 You could extend this study by asking (a) females (b) males to make those judgements. Is there any difference in the way that females and males make judgements about others?

3 Carry out an investigation into implicit personality theories or central character traits. Show two groups a series of photographs which you have cut out of newspapers/magazines and stuck onto a card. Below the photo give a short description of the person in the photo. For Group A, include the word 'warm' in your description, and include the word 'cold' for Group B. Below the description, outline a particular situation, and ask your participants how they think the person in the photo is going to react. Draw any conclusions about implicit personality theories/central character traits from the responses of the two groups, and relate your findings to the work of Asch and Kelley.

Unit Eighteen
Stereotyping and prejudice

This unit deals with the questions

What is the nature of prejudice? How can prejudice be overcome?

Stereotyping is a natural and useful way of helping us to categorise people from what we know of people in general. Sometimes stereotyping turns to prejudice, which can be damaging for individuals and society as a whole.

This unit looks at some explanations of why prejudice develops, how it can lead to discrimination, the effects of discrimination, and how prejudice might be reduced.

The main themes of this topic are:

1 When does stereotyping become prejudice?
2 What are the effects of prejudice?
3 What are the foundations of prejudice?
4 How can prejudice be reduced or overcome?

1 Stereotyping and prejudice

We all tend to put people into categories. In the last unit we looked at implicit personality theories. In this unit we extend that idea to our understanding and explanation of the behaviour of groups.

A stereotype is a view of a person or group based on certain features such as dress, skin colour, physical appearance, size, disability, sex, age, and so on. Stereotyping is natural and useful when we are with people, and helps us to make sensible decisions about how we will relate to them. However, stereotyping can also be too easy and over-simplified, and we sometimes make snap judgements which can be wrong and have lasting damaging effects. Stereotyping may then turn into prejudice. Prejudice is an extreme form of stereotyping.

2 Prejudice and discrimination

An attitude is usually described as a 'relatively permanent disposition towards a person or an event'. Prejudice is an extreme attitude towards others and may be either negative or positive. We may think that all football fans are hooligans and all blonde blue-eyed little girls are angels. This is another example of the halo effect.

Cognitive dissonance

Festinger put forward this theory in 1957, to describe the tension we feel when we have conflicting attitudes, or when the way we behave doesn't match with what we believe - for example, when we smoke even though we know we shouldn't. We try to explain away our behaviour so that one of the conflicting attitudes (and consequently the conflict) will go away. *'What does it matter if I smoke? Other people do, and nothing happens to them.'*

In-groups and out-groups

Positive prejudice may cause us to act in favour of a person. For example, we may like all people who have the same name as ourselves. We would form an in-group. On the other hand, we might not. I might think that they haven't got the right to use my name. So they would form an out-group and I would form the in-group.

Negative prejudice may cause us to act against a person's best interests. People we are prejudiced against would become the out-group. Common forms of prejudice in the West are sexual and racial prejudice. This can often lead to discrimination. *La Piere* (1934) found that some Americans said they were prejudiced when in fact their behaviour didn't match their stated prejudice.

3 The foundations of prejudice

Prejudice seems to have a number of different roots.

1 Group pressure

Pettigrew (1958), among others, investigated the influence of groups and group culture in encouraging prejudice. The very existence of groups seems to encourage a 'them and us' mentality - in-groups and out-groups.

2 Historical reasons

Some groups have come to suffer discrimination for historical reasons. The imperialism of countries like Holland, Britain, France and the US have led some groups such as Blacks to have lower social status. This is the idea of **ethnocentrism** - the belief that one's own group is the norm and the basis from which to judge other groups.

3 Cultural reasons

Within certain cultures, some groups are seen as inferior, such as women and the disabled. Attitudes are often so deeply ingrained in a culture that it is quite difficult for some people even to recognise that they are prejudiced - *'Why do you want a manager's job, anyway? You're only a woman.'*

4 Personality factors

Allport suggested that some personality types are more prone to prejudice than others. ***Dollard et al.*** (1939), for example, found that children who were not allowed to play with attractive toys took out their frustration on the toys they were allowed to play with. ***Dollard et al.*** proposed the **frustration-aggression hypothesis,** when people give vent to their feelings on scapegoats. This is also in line with *Freud's* concept of **displacement,** when people find an object on which to displace their feelings. **Scapegoating theory** can account for a lot of (often socially acceptable) discrimination against groups, such as a lot of Western treatment of Jews and Asians, and almost universal discrimination against physically or mentally disabled persons.

The authoritarian personality
In 1950, ***Adorno and Fraenkle-Brunswick*** proposed the concept that certain personality types were inclined to Fascism. They found a strong relationship between ethnocentrism and Fascism. They discovered that strongly ethnocentric individuals and groups also had inflexible and authoritarian attitudes, rigid disciplinarian views and a generally blinkered view. Adorno coined the term **'the F-scale'**, an instrument for measuring the degree to which people tended to be conformist, obedient, open to regimentation, and inflexible in their views.

5 Media

The media play a big part in setting up and continuing prejudice and discrimination. Messages are communicated specifically or quite subtly about who qualifies as the in-group and who is viewed as inferior.

4 How can prejudice be overcome?

Some psychologists and sociologists have shown that greater integration of groups reduces prejudice. This is particularly effective if groups share similar goals or values, such as in sport or work. ***Deutsch and Collins,*** for example, found that if black and white groups were integrated in housing estates, their prejudice was reduced. If they lived in separate communities, prejudice was strong. **Secord and Blackman** argued that individuals might not discriminate, but the wider groups would.

Sherif (1961) deliberately set groups of 12-year-old boy scouts in competition with each other, but then tried to re-unite them. He found that even though the boys integrated well, they never quite lost their hostility for the other group.

5 Evaluation

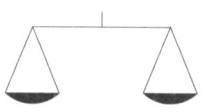

These are very interesting theories which help us to understand why and how people become prejudiced and then discriminate against others, often without realising it. A lot more work needs to be done in psychology and the social sciences in general to help us find ways of reaching understanding of other people, and to work for human improvement.

In your studies, try to relate what you read to your real-life situation. Are you part of a situation in which prejudice is an overt or covert factor? Are you discriminated against? Do you practise discrimination yourself? Why? The main reason for psychological enquiry is to help us understand ourselves and each other better.

6 Summary

What is the nature of prejudice? How can prejudice be overcome?

1 Stereotyping/prejudice
We put people into categories. Categories lead to stereotypes, which can lead to prejudice in extreme form.

2 Prejudice and discrimination
Discrimination comes about through the over-use of prejudice, leading to a 'them and us' situation: in-groups and out-groups.

Cognitive dissonance is a term coined by *Festinger*. It applies to the conflict of attitudes in the same person.

3 Foundations of prejudice
These include the following factors:
- group pressure (***Pettigrew***)
- historical reasons/ethnocentrism
- cultural reasons
- personality factors (authoritarian personality - ***Adorno***);
- displacement theory (***Freud***)
- scapegoating theory
- media

4 Reduction of prejudice
Prejudice can be reduced through -
integration (***Deutsch and Collins***)
limited negotiation (***Secord and Blackman***)
reduction of inter-group conflict (***Sherif***)

7 Now ➡ Over to you...

1 Fill in the missing words

An extreme form of stereotyping is known as p.......................... This can sometimes lead to d.........................., when some people become the ..... -group, and some people become the ....- group.

2 Complete the sentences

(a) Cognitive dissonance means ....
....
(b) Ethnocentrism means ....
....
(c) The authoritarian personality means ....
....

3 Fill in the missing words

Two ways in which prejudice can be overcome is if people (i)..............................
and (ii)..

4 Unscramble the names of these psychologists

Hersif, Llproat, Oodarn, Grewttipe, Stefigner, Dorces, Chsduet, Llodard

5 *From the list, pick out four things that could be the reasons for prejudice*

behaviourism, cognitive dissonance, group pressure, historical reasons, the biosocial approach, maternal deprivation, cultural reasons, monocular cues, personality factors, situational attribution, the Oedipus complex

6 *Which of these sentences are factually correct?*

(a) Prejudice can be overcome if people learn to live together.
(b) Prejudice is an extreme form of stereotyping.
(c) Ethnocentrism describes an attitude that says that some people are entitled to make judgements about others.
(d) Cognitive dissonance happens when our actions live up to our beliefs.
(e) Sherif got boy scouts to be in competition with each other, and then tried to bring them together again.

8 Written exercises

1 What is the difference between stereotyping and prejudice? Give two examples from your own experience.
2 What is ethnocentrism?
3 Give two examples of cognitive dissonance and how people try to resolve it.
4 What are the main reasons for prejudice?
5 How do the media contribute to the continuation of certain kinds of prejudice?
6 How might prejudice be overcome?

9 Topics for discussion

1 You are a governor of a school serving various ethnic groups. Drawing on your knowledge of psychology, outline some of the policies you might introduce to avoid or reduce potential discrimination.

2 You are a manager of a business. How would you ensure that females and males had equal and full entitlement?

3 What are the advantages and disadvantages of competitive sports and other practices?

10 Need to know

▱ Can you explain how stereotyping can be useful, but can become damaging if carried to extremes?

▱ Can you explain how discrimination might be caused?

▱ Can you outline psychological theories about the foundations of prejudice?

▱ Can you explain how prejudice might be overcome?

▱ Can you name all the psychologists mentioned in this unit, and describe their work?

▱ Can you relate the studies here to real life examples?

11 Suggestions for coursework

1 Carry out a survey into public opinion about stereotyping and prejudice. In particular, investigate whether people feel that stereotyping is useful or harmful, and whether prejudice is useful or harmful.

2 Carry out an observational study into discrimination by observing people's reactions to others in so-called 'inferior' positions. For example, observe shop assistants, or cleaners, or waiters/waitresses. Using categories of behaviour, note how often people use patronising terms such as 'dear', 'my man', 'Oi! You!', etc., or speak in a superior way. What does this tell you about attitudes in our society? (Make sure that you get permission to carry out your study if necessary.)

More challenging studies

1 Carry out an investigation into cognitive dissonance. Identify a group of people who are smokers. Give them a questionnaire asking them why they smoke. Give them a handout explaining the health hazards of smoking, and offering practical advice about how they can stop. With their full permission (of course), contact them a month later. Give them a questionnaire asking if they have given up smoking, and, if not, why not. Using the results from your two questionnaires, draw you own conclusions regarding how people attempt to resolve cognitive dissonance, and relate it to the work of Festinger.

2 Carry out a survey into attitudes to a particular minority group. Give people a questionnaire asking if they are prejudiced against this group (e.g. people who are tattooed), and also asking about their behaviour when they are in contact with this group (would they employ someone with tattoos, for example). See if the two sets of responses actually match, or if people who say they are not prejudiced actually do discriminate.

Unit Nineteen
Social influence

This unit deals with the questions

What influence do other people have on us?
Does our behaviour change when we are with other people?
If so, why does it?

Who am I?
Is the real me the person that I am when I am by myself, or does the real me emerge when I am with other people?
Am I simply playing a role?
Could it even be that I am playing a role no matter what situation I am in?

There is little doubt that most of us change our behaviour, and perhaps role - even perhaps our personality - when we are in the company of others.

The main themes in this topic are

1 What effect does an audience have on our behaviour?
2 When do we intervene as bystanders, and why do we (or not, as the case may be)?
3 What influence do other people have on the role we play?

1 Audience effects

Our behaviour is often influenced by the presence of others (**audience effects**). This was first investigated by *Triplett* in 1898 who compared the rate of performance of children by themselves when they were doing everyday tasks with their rate of performance when they were with others. He found that children tended to perform faster when they were with others. Being influenced by the presence of other people is called '**social facilitation**'.

The presence of an audience can have different effects, which are usually like this:

If I am good at something, I will perform even better with an audience because I feel confident.
If I am weak at something, I will perform poorly with an audience because I will feel unsure and inhibited.

Our performance level - improved performance or worsened performance - is our **dominant response.**

Studies

Allport (1923) investigated the **co-action effect** - when people knew they were performing the same task but did not necessarily interact with each other, such as doing individual exams in the same room. It appears that knowing that others are occupied in the same way encourages us to work faster, although quality suffers on harder tasks.

Zajonc, in the 1960s, suggested that an audience increases an individual's level of arousal, which improves task performance on easy tasks but lowers task performance on more difficult ones (see also the Yerkes-Dodson law, Unit 9.).

2 Bystander intervention

If there are a number of people at the scene of an accident we would expect most people to help. In fact the reverse seems to be true. The more people there are, the fewer seem to want to help. Lack of intervention is called **bystander apathy.**

Factors preventing bystander intervention

1 Diffusion of responsibility

A well known study by ***Latané and Darley*** (1968), investigating the Kitty Genovese murder, showed that not one of the 38 people who observed her murder attempted to call the police at the time because they thought someone else would do so. This is called diffusion of responsibility, when everyone assumes that someone else will do something.

2 Presence of other people

Latané and Rodin investigated this in a study where a person waited in a room, but in the room next door a secretary pretended to fall and cried out. People waiting alone or with a friend tended to go to her assistance while people waiting with a stranger in the room didn't.

3 Defining the situation

In another experiment, **Latané and Darley** arranged for smoke to billow into a room from under a door. 75% of people waiting alone reported it, while only 10% of those waiting with strangers did. It appears that the greatest problem with intervention is the fear of looking silly in other people's eyes. People seem prepared literally to die of embarrassment!

Latané and Darley suggested that if people defined the situation for themselves (perhaps as an emergency) they would act; otherwise they would go along with the group attitude towards the situation in deciding whether it was important or not.

Factors encouraging bystander intervention

1 Modelling

Bryan and Test (1967) explored how behaviour could be **modelled.** They set up a motorway study to see whether motorists stopped to help another motorist who had broken down if they had seen someone else doing the same thing just a little time before. The results showed that, out of the motorists who did stop, those who had seen someone helping a breakdown a little while before tended to stop and help, while those who had not seen the 'model' beforehand tended not to stop.

2 Altruism

Piliavin found that people would help someone who appeared to be ill 95% of the time, and 50% of the time even if the person appeared to be drunk. People genuinely appeared to want to help.

3 What influence do other people have on the role we play?

Social norms

When we are with other people we usually feel we have to fall into a particular role according to other people's expectations. We all play multiple roles each day, and speak the lines that each social situation demands. These are social norms - that is, the normal behaviour that society expects and demands. If we break the rules we run into problems and have to bear the consequences. These can often take the form of punishments or sanctions. We internalise (learn and accept) cultural and social norms from birth.

Roles

Linton (1945) identified 5 different social groupings, each with its own roles and role behaviour:

> age and sex roles - old man, young girl
> family roles - mother, father, child
> status roles - manager, worker
> occupational roles - teacher, nurse, shopkeeper
> common interest grouping roles - golfer, gardener

Role and personality

Zimbardo et al. (1973) set up a 'prison' study in the basement of Stanford University, where students were invited to role play being guards or prisoners. The study had to stop after six days as both 'guards' and 'prisoners' internalised their roles so well that they came to see this as real life. This experiment suggests that role has not much to do with personality.

Factors encouraging certain kinds of behaviour appear to be **role expectation,** where we tend to act in the way thought to be normal for that role, and **de-individuation,** where people feel that they have lost their personal identity and become one of the crowd.

Self-fulfilling prophecy

Sometimes we fill a role, even for a short time, and then people come to expect us to fill that role and assume that we will always behave in that particular way. If we do, the prophecy is fulfilled - for example, someone tells me they think I am musical, so I practise hard at my music and therefore become very good at it.

The idea of role and role behaviour is essential to the next unit on group behaviour (Unit 20), involving conformity, obedience and compliance.

4 Evaluation

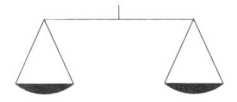

This area of study has real significance for our image of who we are and why we think and behave as we do. Do we think and act because we believe certain things and want to act in particular ways, or are we conditioned by social norms and expectations? Is our thinking itself socially conditioned?

Who are we? Are we the persons that we are, or are we the persons that other people expect us to be? Where does our freedom lie? Have we in fact any freedom, either of thinking or action? Freedom seems meaningless in the light of social influence, which indicates that we are, in everything we do, the result of other people's ideas and wishes.

As well as these issues, there is another one about being prepared to adopt certain roles that we are expected to play. Sometimes it is much more comfortable to behave according to social expectations, than to decide to go our own way. What price are we prepared to pay for this? Being the person we want to be rather than the person other people want us to be can sometimes be expensive in the light of what we get back from other people. Consider what might happen if you wore the clothes you best like to your place of work or study; or if you really did what you wanted to do, or said the things you really thought. Could you do this without running the risk of other people's disapproval? Success in life is often tied in with meeting other people's role expectations of us, and their expectations of us might be different from our own.

You might apply these questions to yourself and your friends, to check the way you think about things, and how you can relate real life experiences to the work you are studying.

5 Summary

What influence do other people have on us? Does our behaviour change when we are with other people? If so, why does it?

1 Audience effects
Key concepts here are:
- social facilitation is being influenced by the presence of others;
- dominant response is how we respond to being observed by others;
- co-action effect *(Allport)* is what can happen when people are working individually on a task in the company of others;
- increased motivation to succeed (*Zajonc*) is what can happen when we have an audience.

2 Bystander intervention
Factors preventing intervention (causing apathy)
- diffusion of responsibility
- presence of other people
- defining the situation

Factors encouraging intervention (causing interest)
- modelling
- altruism

3 Social role
Social norms are the normal behaviour society expects and demands.

Linton identified five role groupings
- age and sex
- family status
- occupational
- status
- common interest

Zimbardo found that there was little relationship between role and personality

4 Self-fulfilling prophecy
When we act in the way that other people believe we should or will act, this is called the self-fulfilling prophecy - that is, the prophecy they make about us is fulfilled.

6 Now ➡ Over to you...

1 *Complete the following sentences about audience effects*

(a) If I am good at something, an audience will make me ....
....
(b) If I am weak at something, an audience will make me ....
....

2 *Match the names of the psychologists with the studies*

(a) Zimbardo	(i)	explored how behaviour could be modelled by setting up the motorway breakdown situation
(b) Zajonc	(ii)	found that people genuinely wanted to help others
(c) Latané and Darley	(iii)	investigated the co-action effect, of people doing the same task but not necessarily interacting with each other
(d) Latané and Rodin	(iv)	investigated the effects that an audience had on an individual's levels of arousal
(e) Bryan and Test	(v)	investigated the Kitty Genovese murder to see why people did not get involved in situations

172 *Interpersonal Processes*

(f) Piliavin   (vi)   investigated bystander apathy amongst people in a waiting room who heard a cry for help from the room next door

(g) Latané and Rodin (again)   (vii)   arranged for smoke to billow into a waiting room to see people's reactions if they were alone, with friends, or among strangers

(h) Allport   (viii)   set up a 'prison' experiment to test people's willingness to take on roles

3 *Fill in the missing words*

(a) There are three main factors that prevent bystander intervention. They are d.............. of ...., pr.................. of other p................, and d.................. the s..................

(b) There are two main factors that encourage bystander intervention. They are m.................. and a..................

4 *Match the role with the role group*

(a) age and sex roles   (i)   teacher, nurse, shopkeeper
(b) family roles   (ii)   old man, young girl
(c) status roles   (iii)   mother, father, child
(d) occupational roles   (iv)   golfer, gardener
(e) common interest roles   (v)   manager, worker

6   Written exercises

1 When might our performance at a task be improved or negatively affected by the presence of other people?
2 What factors appear to prevent bystander intervention, and what factors appear to encourage it? Draw on psychological studies to support your argument.
3 What influence do other people have on the role we play?
4 What kinds of social roles do we usually occupy?
5 From your reading and experience of life in general, give 3 examples (fictitious or factual) of the self-fulfilling prophecy.

7 Topics for discussion

1. Do you think personality and role sometimes get confused? Have we actually got a real identity, or do we simply trot out the person we think we ought to be for a particular situation?

2. Do you think that the studies of Bryan and Piliavin would still be valid today, or would social norms have changed so that we would be cautious about stopping on a motorway to help an apparently distressed motorist, or a collapsed person on the underground?

8 Need to know

- Can you say what effect an audience has on our behaviour?
- Can you say what factors influence bystander apathy and bystander intervention?
- Can you identify the kinds of social role groupings that Linton suggested?
- Can you explain the difference between role and personality?
- Can you describe the effect of the self-fulfilling prophecy?
- Can you name all the psychologists mentioned in this unit, and describe their work?

9 Suggestions for coursework

Note: When undertaking coursework in this topic, it is very tempting to set up a situation in which a person plays a stooge to test the effects of bystander intervention or apathy. For GCSE work you should NOT attempt this.

1 Carry out an experiment into audience effects. Arrange three groups, Group A, Group B and Group C. You will have to work with the three groups at different times. Give all groups the same, fairly simple physical task to do, such as stacking dominoes or cutting out shapes from paper. Record the time each participant takes to do the set task. Arrange for the individuals in Group A to undertake this task in isolation, with no audience. Arrange for the individuals in Group B to undertake this task together. Arrange for the individuals in Group C to undertake

this task together, and with a larger audience - perhaps the whole class. Compare the timings of all individuals and all groups, and draw your own conclusions about how the presence of others might facilitate our performance.

More challenging studies

1 Carry out an observational study of bystander intervention or apathy in a supermarket or other public place. Watch when a person is in some difficulty, such as dropping items of shopping from a trolley, or not coping very well with a lot of luggage at an airport. Observe whether other people come to help. Observe what their situation is - whether they are alone, or with friends. Draw your own conclusions about the circumstances in which we seem ready or reluctant to be involved in other people's affairs. You will need to draw up categories of behaviour for individuals, and also note if they are alone or in company. (By the way, what would you do while you were observing?)

2 Carry out a survey into bystander intervention. Give people a text to read about the Kitty Genovese murder, and ask them why they thought the people who observed her murder were reluctant to act. Ask your participants if they feel this reaction is true to life, or if other factors might have been involved. Ask your participants if they would have acted in the same way or differently. Draw your own conclusions, based on your study of psychology, about the ability of people to overcome social pressures and expectations. You might also consider, depending on your participants' answers, whether we all have the ability to fool ourselves! (Remember to assure your participants that you will preserve their anonymity.)

Unit Twenty
Group pressures

This unit looks at the influence of groups on individuals. The unit deals with the questions

What kind of influence do people have on individuals' behaviour?
What do people do to make individuals conform to group norms?

Many people think that, in order for society to work smoothly, people have to agree certain 'norms', that is, behave in certain ways that are accepted by the majority. Certain pressures are applied to make sure that individuals do conform to the norms. Group norms are often kept through the compliance, conformity and obedience of individuals.

The main themes of this topic are

1 The idea of group norms
2 How individuals are persuaded to adopt group attitudes
3 Ethical considerations of studies which investigate these

1 The idea of group norms

As we saw in the previous unit, norms (from the word normal) refer to the behaviour and attitudes that a group expect from individuals. If an individual behaves or thinks in a way different from the majority, s/he runs the risk of sanctions. These can be as mild as social disapproval - perhaps people will laugh if I walk down the street in my pyjamas; but they can also be severe - perhaps I will be put into prison if I steal other people's possessions.

Group norms should not be confused with **group rules.** Rules refer to an agreed system to make sure that a group runs smoothly, whether it is large or small. Norms refer to attitudes and behaviours, and how people play out their given role, or act correctly.

2 How individuals are persuaded to adopt group attitudes

If an individual is not behaving 'correctly', the rest of us try to persuade the person to come into line. We expect the person to **comply** with a request, to **conform** to our expectations, or to **obey** an order. It is difficult for people to resist social persuasion.

Kelman (1958) argues that there are 3 levels of social influence:

1 **compliance** - when a person goes along with the majority but does not change their attitudes;
2 **internalisation** - when a person changes their personal beliefs because they think another view is better;
3 **identification** - when a person actively tries to be like someone else they admire.

Note: When we comply, conform and obey, this can refer only to our behaviour. We do not necessarily change our attitude towards a situation, but simply act in a certain way. All the studies referred to below demonstrate compliance, but some show a greater degree of compliance which then turns into conformity or obedience.

Studies in conformity

The most well-known studies are by *Asch* (1951). He arranged for one person to be in the company of a group of stooges who all agreed that two lines, actually of different lengths, were of the same length. 74% of the participants agreed with the majority at some time. 32% conformed all the time.

Perrin and Spencer (1980) replicated the experiments and found similar results only when the people involved already were in an authoritarian relationship, such as young offenders on probation with probation officers. They argued that since the 1950s, the general population had grown more self-assured and were less willing to conform.

It appears that most people do conform frequently to group expectations for fear of embarrassment at being seen as the odd one out. It is interesting that the presence of allies can reduce the conformity effect. We seem to need three people offering opposing views to us in order to conform, but even only one ally will encourage us not to conform.

Studies in obedience

Milgram (1963) required people to deliver 'electric shocks' to a 'learner' when the 'learner' responded incorrectly to a stimulus. The learner was a stooge. Many people delivered 'shocks' of increasing severity, even over the stated danger level.

Factors encouraging obedience seemed to be

> **social contract**, where the participants felt they had agreed to carry out the experiment;
> **role expectation,** where the experimenter was perceived to be an authority figure;
> **abdication of responsibility,** where the participants felt that they were 'only obeying orders'.

Hofling (1966) expected nurses to break safety regulations under the orders of a doctor. 50% of nurses obeyed the doctors. Although practices in hospitals have changed a lot since the 1960s, so that such a situation would not be possible today, the principles involved of people obeying authority figures may well still apply.

3 Ethical considerations

It is doubtful whether the suffering and anguish experienced by participants in studies like those conducted by Milgram, Hofling and Zimbardo justify them in the name of understanding human behaviour. A number of the participants in the studies had to receive counselling. The psychologists involved claimed that they fully de-briefed their participants, and assured them of anonymity. Milgram said that a high proportion of the participants said they were glad they had taken part in the experiment.

4 Evaluation

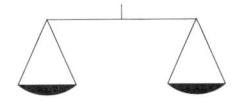

These studies can be very disturbing for our views of individual liberty and identity. They suggest that we tend to conform to group expectations for fear of being seen as the odd one out. It is very important for us to feel comfortable with others, and so we might give up some of our more unusual or stronger ideas for a quiet life, particularly if those ideas are not in the majority or even unpopular.

There is an important issue here about individual liberty, particularly as it applies to what might be called 'deviance'. Anyone who acts out of keeping with role expectation might be called a deviant. How does society try to control deviants and bring them back into line with social expectations? What happens when people want to exert their individuality and break with social convention? What sort of penalties do independent people pay for their right to exercise their individuality?

You might ask yourself and your friends these questions, to check the way you think about things, and see how you can relate real life experiences to the work you are studying.

5 Summary

What kind of influence do people have on individuals' behaviour? What do people do to make individuals conform to group norms?

1 Group norms

How do social expectations influence and determine the roles that people play?

2 Persuasion to adopt group attitudes

What levels of persuasion are there? How can people be persuaded to meet social expectations? There are different degrees to which people are prepared to meet group expectations.

Kelman's categorisations
   compliance
   internalisation
   identification

Studies
   Conformity - *Asch, Perrin and Spencer*
   Obedience - *Milgram, Hofling*

3 Ethical issues

Can advances in understanding compensate for distress caused to individuals in carrying out these studies?

6 Now ➡ Over to you...

1 *Fill in the missing words*

Kelman said that there were three levels of social influence. They were c........................., i............................. and i...

2 *Match the word with the description*

(a) compliance   (i)   when a person changes their personal beliefs because they think another view is better

(b) internalisation (ii) when a person actively tries to be like someone else whom they admire

(c) identification   (iii) when a person goes along with the majority but does not change their attitude

3 *Match the psychologists with the descriptions*

(a) Asch   (i)   got participants to deliver 'electric shocks' to a 'learner'
(b) Perrin and Spencer (ii) got nurses to break safety regulations
(c) Milgram   (iii) got people to talk about things that they didn't see
(d) Hofling   (iv) said that people in the 1980s were more aware and confident

4 *Choose the correct word from the list given*

(a) If someone asks me to stand up, and I do, I comply/conform/obey.
(b) If I stand up because everyone else is standing up, I comply/conform/obey.
(c) If someone tells me to stand up, and I do, I comply/conform/obey.

7 Written exercises

1 What are group norms?
2 What can happen to people who do not conform to group norms?
3 What are the differences between compliance, conformity and obedience?
4 Briefly outline the studies in conformity of Asch, and Perrin and Spencer.
5 Compare and contrast the studies of Milgram and Hofling.
6 What ethical considerations are there in the work of Milgram and Hofling?

Interpersonal Processes

8 Topics for discussion

1. Do you feel people should conform to group expectations? Is there any justification for unusual behaviour? Give reasons for and against.

2. Would you agree that the ends justify the means in studies such as those of Milgram and Hofling?

3. From your knowledge of psychology, explain how individuals are persuaded to accept social norms.

4. You are in a managerial position. From your knowledge of psychology, explain how you might get people to behave in a way that suited your particular policy.

9 Need to know

- Can you explain what the idea of group norms involves?
- Can you explain the difference between compliance, conformity and obedience?
- Can you describe Kelman's three levels of social influence and how individuals are persuaded to adopt group attitudes?
- Can you describe studies in conformity and obedience?
- Can you identify what would persuade people to go along with a situation or activity with which they basically disagreed?
- Can you talk about the ethical considerations in the work described in this unit and others?
- Can you name all the psychologists in this unit, and describe their work?

10 Suggestions for coursework

Note: You must never use stooges in GCSE coursework. You must never put people in a position of feeling uncomfortable or embarrassed. There are very serious ethical issues here.

1 Conduct an observational study of the queuing behaviour at a self-service cafe, supermarket or motorway service area. Compare the behaviour of different sex or age groups, or people alone or with others. Use categories of behaviour for your different groups.

2 Conduct a non-participant observation of who is most likely to put money into charity boxes in a busy shopping area. Decide on several groups, perhaps different sex or age groups, or people alone or with others, or adults with children, or older people, and observe the behaviour of people in these groups. You might draw up a hypothesis about whether some groups are more altruistic than others.

More challenging studies

1 Carry out an observational study of any social situation in a public place. Observe how people tend to conform to group norms and expectations. For example, in supermarkets we are very obedient about standing in queues. What happens when someone tries to jump the queue, say in a supermarket or other shop? You could extend this study to show how people deal with those who break the rules. Have you ever observed the attitudes of British people to foreigners who are not accustomed to queuing in their country, and who innocently break the rules in Britain? Sometimes the sanctions can be quite severe!

2 Carry out a survey into attitudes towards unusual people. Try to find out how people regard others who behave in an unusual way. When does idiosyncracy become deviance? What about public opinion - when does amused tolerance become anger and hostility? For example, people tend to go along with a certain amount of unconventional dress but get quite hostile at extreme forms of dress.

Part Three
Worked papers

As you have read in Part One, the NEAB GCSE Psychology examination will operate at two levels: Option P, which is well within the grasp of most candidates, and Option Q, which is pitched at a slightly more demanding level. You need to know in advance which level you are going to aim for. You cannot enter for both levels.

In this section, you will find pointers about how the examinations are set and marked. On pages 186-199, you will see sample questions, with comments about the level at which they are pitched, and with guidance about the marking schemes. On pages 200-218 you will see actual specimen papers for the revised 1996 syllabus. You will see specimen papers, for both Option P and Option Q, often using the same stimulus material, but showing how the questions that are set will vary according to level of difficulty, and how the marking scheme will be adjusted to the level.

Now please look at the sample material which follows. You will see that the questions always follow a similar format: there is some stimulus material, followed by several structured questions. In the sample material, we have indicated which level is appropriate, and the marks that would be allocated for those questions. We have supplied model answers, but we would stress that these are not the only answers, although student answers should roughly be along these lines.

Here are some general points.

❑ Every question, whether for Option P or for Option Q, will follow a structured format. The questions will start easier and grow progressively more difficult.

❑ You will never be asked about anything which is not specified in the syllabus. This does not mean, however, that you should skip parts of psychology courses that are not geared specifically to the syllabus. The syllabus is a minimum requirement only.

❑ Questions for Option P and Option Q tend to be worded differently. Option P, for example, asks you questions such as 'Describe a study ... '. The questions ask only for basic knowledge of the study. Option Q asks you questions such as 'Describe and evaluate a study ... '. The questions ask for your insights and critical evaluation, as well as your basic knowledge of the study.

❑ You are expected to know studies which are described in the literature. When you read the instructions in the examination to 'Describe one study ... ', this means that you must describe a study that you have read in the literature. You must not make up one of your own.

❑ Don't worry if you don't know or don't write down the names of psychologists who conducted the study (although it is obviously better if you do). You are marked positively in this examination - that is, you are marked for the knowledge that you show. You are not asked for names of psychologists, so you should not worry that you will lose marks if you don't know the names. In the same way, if you say the wrong name of a psychologist, you will not be marked down. This means that you can write freely, without fear that you will lose marks because you cannot remember names.

❑ In the same way, you are not expected to know the dates of studies, although it is useful for you to know them for your general knowledge about psychology, and be able to compare, say, one study with another at a particular time.

❑ In questions that ask you to describe a particular study, you will see that the marking scheme operates something like this:

    basic method (1 mark)
    accurate method (2 marks)
        +
    results (1 mark)
    difference (1 mark)
    outcome (1 mark)
    direction (1 mark)
    evaluation (1 mark)

The number of marks allocated may vary, and the wording may also vary. The marking scheme would probably not contain all of these assessment criteria, only a selection.

The interpretation for the marking scheme is this:

- ❖ **basic method**: this requires you to give an outline of the study.
- ❖ **accurate method**: this requires you to give an accurate account of the study.
- ❖ **results**: this requires you to say what the results of the study were.
- ❖ **difference**: this requires you to say what the differences were between the people or groups who were taking part in the study.
- ❖ **outcome**: this is the outcome of the study (similar to results).
- ❖ **direction**: this requires you to say where the results were pointed: i.e. whether the relationship stated in the original hypothesis was supported or rejected. In simple terms, this means whether the study showed a significant change in people's attitudes or behaviour in a certain direction.
- ❖ **evaluation**: this requires you to give your opinion about the method, outcomes or other aspects of the study, and to point out its strengths and weaknesses where appropriate, or to compare it with other studies which might have different results or start with different hypotheses.

❏ Look carefully at the number of marks awarded for each answer. This usually gives you an indication of how many points you need to make in your answer.

❏ You will find some questions that ask you to 'Discuss a study'. You are required to

    (a) describe the study;
    (b) say what the outcome was;
    (c) give an evaluation.

❏ In the sample material, under every question you will see the level at which the question is pitched:

either (Options P and Q)
or   (Option Q only)

This means that (Options P and Q) refers to questions that are appropriate to both Options P and Q, but (Option Q only) refers to questions that are appropriate to Option Q only.

❏ In the specimen papers (pages 200-218) you will see how the examination questions are laid out, with room for you to write the answer in. In the sample material there is no space for written answers. The purpose of the sample material is to give advice on the kinds of marking schemes that are used.

Example 1

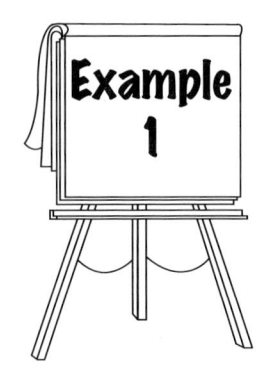

In the Christmas play, child A, who was renowned for her acting ability, was given the starring role. Child B, a shy, timid little girl, was given a supporting role. The parents of child B saw this as an opportunity for her to learn to become more confident, and encouraged her, months before the play, to believe that she could do really well. On the night of the play, child B began marvellously, but then, half way through, she forgot her lines. Her performance disintegrated after that. Child A continued to turn in a stunning performance.

1 This episode could be seen as an example of the self-fulfilling prophecy. What is 'the self-fulfilling prophecy'? (3 marks)
(Options P and Q)

Answer A statement/belief (1 mark) which comes true (1 mark) because it has been made/expected (1 mark). (Total 3 marks)

2 What do we mean by 'audience effect'? (2 marks)
(Options P and Q)

Answer Performance in a task varies (1 mark) if there are others present (1 mark). (Total 2 marks)

3 The reactions to audience effect by child A and child B were fairly typical of people's responses. What can you say about audience effect in terms of anticipated effects on individual performance? (4 marks)
(Option Q only)

Answer If you are good at something (1 mark) you will perform even better with an audience (1 mark) (Total 2 marks)
If you are weak at something (1 mark) you will perform worse with an audience (1 mark) (Total 2 marks)

4 What do we mean by 'bystander intervention'? (1 mark)
(Options P and Q)

Answer: The readiness to help someone in need of assistance (1 mark)

5 Name two factors involved in bystander apathy (2 marks)
(Options P and Q

Answer any two of the following:
    The number of people present (1 mark)
    Relationship with the other(s) present (1 mark)
    Defining the situation as an emergency (1 mark) (Total 2 marks)

6(a) From your knowledge of psychology, describe one study that showed the outcomes of bystander effect. (3 marks)
(Options P and Q)

Answer   basic description of study   (1 mark)
             accurate description of study   (1 mark)
             +
             outcome   (1 mark)   (Total 3 marks)

6(b) From your knowledge of psychology, describe and evaluate one study that showed the outcomes of bystander effect. (5 marks)
(Option Q only)

Answer   basic description of study   (1 mark)
             accurate description of study   (2 marks)
             +
             results: difference   (1 mark)
                        direction   (1 mark)
                        evaluation point   (1 mark)

                        (any combination for 5 marks)   (Total 5 marks)

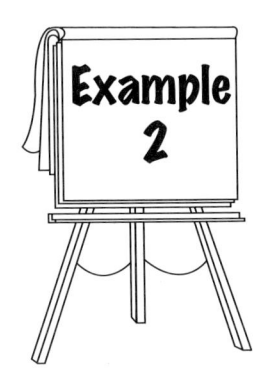

Example 2

1 What name do we give to the phenomenon that lets us see the following images as showing the same object?

(a)

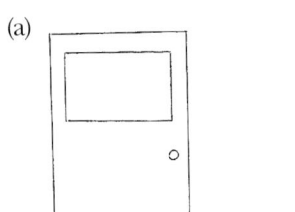

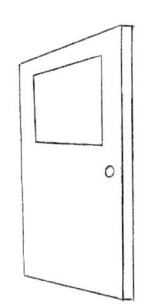

(1 mark)

(b)

(1 mark)

(Options P and Q)

Answers   (a) size constancy   (1 mark)
              (b) shape constancy   (1 mark)   (Total 2 marks)

2 What is the difference between monocular and binocular depth cues? (2 marks)
(Options P and Q)

Answer   monocular - an indication of distance which can be detected with one eye   (1 mark)
binocular - an indication of distance requiring two eyes   (1 mark)
(Total 2 marks)

3(a) From your knowledge of psychology, describe any one study that shows that perception might be innate .   (4 marks)
(Options P and Q)

Answer   basic method   (1 mark) or
accurate method   (2 marks)
+
results   (1 mark)
direction   (1 mark)   (Total 4 marks)

3(b) From your knowledge of psychology, describe and evaluate any one study that shows that perception might be innate.   (5 marks)
(Option Q only)

Answer   basic method   (1 mark) or
accurate method   (2 marks)
+
results   (1 mark)
direction   (1 mark)
evaluation   (1 mark)   (Total 5 marks)

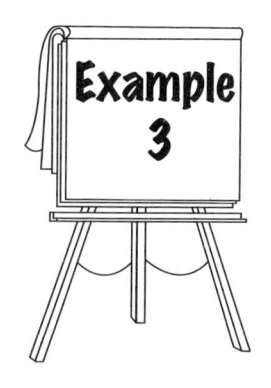

Example 3

Jane taught her puppy Buster to sit at the kerb by giving him one of his favourite chocolates whenever he obeyed her command to sit. Now, when they approach the edge of a pavement, Buster sits even without Jane's command.

1 From the situation described, and using your knowledge of operant conditioning, say what reinforcement is.   (1 mark)
(Options P and Q)

Answer   Something which strengthens a learned response   (1 mark)

2 Why should Jane continue to reward Buster's good behaviour occasionally?
(Options P and Q) (2 marks)

Answer Occasional reinforcement (1 mark) to avoid extinction of conditioned response (1 mark). (Total 2 marks)

3 Jane could have shaped Buster's behaviour using operant conditioning. From your knowledge of schedules of reinforcement, which two schedules should Jane use to train Buster which would be most resistant to extinction? (2 marks)
(Option Q only)

Answer variable - interval (1 mark)
variable - ratio (1 mark) (Total 2 marks)

4 With reference to your knowledge of psychological theory, describe two similarities and two differences between classical and operant conditioning.
(Option Q only) (4 marks)

Answer differences:
(a) operant conditioning is more complex than classical (1 mark)
(b) operant conditioning deals with voluntary actions rather than reflexes (1 mark)
similarities:
(a) both link behaviour to a stimulus of some kind (1 mark)
(b) both have been investigated mainly by using animals (1 mark)
or any other correct statement (1 mark) (Maximum 4 marks)

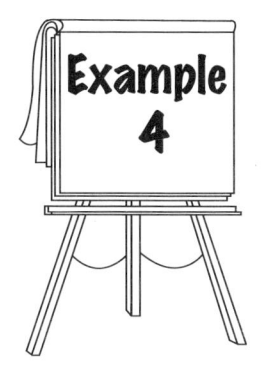

Example 4

Two groups each of 10 students were given a list of 20 words to learn.

The first group was presented with the list of words with no particular format:

dog, orange, violin, chair, oboe, apple, cat, wardrobe, table, flute, rhinoceros, lemon, horse, pineapple, bed, guitar, settee, accordion, cow, banana

The second group was presented with the list of words arranged under category headings:

animals	musical instruments	pieces of furniture	fruit
dog	violin	table	banana
cat	oboe	bed	orange
rhinoceros	flute	wardrobe	apple
horse	guitar	settee	lemon
cow	accordion	chair	pineapple

The following day, both groups were asked to recall the list of words. The results were as follows:

	Average number of words recalled correctly
Group 1	10
Group 2	18

1 Write a hypothesis for this study. (1 mark)
(Options P and Q)

Answer Memory will be better if the material is organised (1 mark)
(or any other appropriate hypothesis)

2 State the independent variable and the dependent variable in this study.
(Options P and Q) (2 marks)

Answer independent variable - presentation format (1 mark)
dependent variable - number of words recalled correctly (1 mark)
(do not allow 'results') (Total 2 marks)

3 Name one variable that has not been controlled in the presentation of the two lists. (1 mark)
(Options P and Q)

Answer length of word, number of syllables, timing, etc. (1 mark)

3 From these findings, what can be said about the effect of category headings on recall? (2 marks)
(Options P and Q)

Answer improving organisation on the list at the input stage (1 mark)
will lead to better recall (1 mark) (Total 2 marks)

4(a) Describe a study that investigates perceptual defence. (4 marks)
(Options P and Q)

Answer basic method   (1 mark)
accurate method   (2 marks)
results - difference (1 mark)
         direction   (1 mark)   (maximum 4 marks)

4(b) Describe and evaluate a study that investigates perceptual defence (5 marks)
(Option Q only)

Answer basic method   (1 mark)
accurate method   (2 marks)
results   (1 mark)
difference   (1 mark)
direction   (1 mark)
evaluation   (1 mark)   (maximum 5)

5 Discuss one ethical issue associated with this study   (3 marks)
(Options P and Q)

Answer naming the issue   (1 mark)
its effect   (1 mark)
ways to deal with it (1 mark)   (maximum 3 marks)

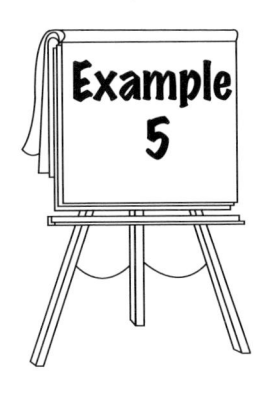

Example 5

A psychologist wanted to find out whether the amount of reading that childen undertook in school was related to the quality of their creative writing. From a class of 20 children, she asked 12 to be participants. They were each asked to keep a record of how much reading they undertook in school each week, and were then asked to write an imaginative essay at the end of each week. Each child was given a mark out of 20 for the term's work. The investigation lasted for ten weeks.

The following table shows the results of her experiment.

Child	Amount of reading in hours per week	Mark for term
A	6	15
B	8	15
C	10	18
D	4	12
E	8	16
F	11	19
G	11	18
H	8	12
I	9	17
J	10	17
K	19	20
L	7	14

All questions for
(Options P and Q)

1 How many participants took part? (1 mark)

Answer 12 (1 mark)

2 Write down the hypothesis for this study. (2 marks)

Answer There is a relationship between the number of hours spent reading each week (1 mark) and the number of marks earned at the end of term (1 mark). (Total 2 marks)

3 On the graph paper, plot the data, showing the amount of reading undertaken by individual students and the marks they obtained. Fully label your graph.
(5 marks)

Answer title (1 mark)
axes labelled (2 marks)
accurate plotting (1 mark)
appropriate use of graph paper (1 mark) (Total 5 marks)

4 What kind of relationship does the graph show? (2 marks)

Answer positive (1 mark) correlation (1 mark) (Total 2 marks)

Sample questions and specimen papers 193

5(a) Suggest two variables that the psychologist should have controlled. (2 marks)

Answer
(i) any participant variable (1 mark)
(ii) environmental conditions (1 mark)
(iii) any other relevant variable (1 mark) (maximum 2 marks)

5(b) How could she have controlled these variables? (4 marks)

Answer
(i) information from school/home (1 mark) before selecting sample (1 mark) (Total 2 marks)
(ii) instruct parents to make sure that all reading for the week is done in a quiet, well-lit room (2 marks)
(iii) any other reasonable attempt (2 marks) (Maximum 4 marks)

6 State two criticisms of this type of investigation. (4 marks)
(Option Q only)

Answer no manipulation of independent variable (2 marks)
cause and effect cannot be ascertained (2 marks) (Total 4 marks)

Example 6

A psychology student wanted to find out if TV advertising reinforced traditional sex-role images. She watched TV advertisements during a one hour period at the same time every evening for a week. She identified certain categories of behaviour that she felt were typical of sex-role stereotypes, and kept a record of how many instances she observed of males and females fulfilling these roles. Here is her record sheet.

	Monday	Tuesday	Wednesday	Thursday	Friday	Saturday	Sunday
Domestic role e.g. washing up							
female	⊞ IIII	II	⊞	⊞ I	II	⊞ I	⊞ II
male	I	III	II	I		III	
DIY role e.g. mending, fixing plugs, etc.							
female	III	I			II	IIII	⊞
male	⊞ III	⊞ I	⊞ II	⊞	⊞ II	⊞	⊞ IIII

	Monday	Tuesday	Wednesday	Thursday	Friday	Saturday	Sunday
Care-giver role e.g. looking after children							
female	⫽⫽⫽ III	⫽⫽⫽	⫽⫽⫽ II	⫽⫽⫽ ⫽⫽⫽	IIII	IIII I	IIII III
male	I	II		I	II	I	IIII
Head of the household role e.g. planning family holiday							
female	II	III	II	IIII	I	II	I
male	⫽⫽⫽ II	⫽⫽⫽ II	IIII	⫽⫽⫽ III	⫽⫽⫽	III	⫽⫽⫽ I

1 What kind of study is this called? (1 mark)
(Options P and Q)

Answer An observation study (1 mark)

2 What is meant by time sampling? (2 marks)
(Options P and Q)

Answer Selecting equal sized units of time (1 mark) throughout a given period to conduct observations (1 mark) (Total 2 marks)

3 Name any two variables that the psychologist should have controlled, and how she could have controlled them. (4 marks)
(Options P and Q)

Answer Variable (i) observer bias (1 mark)
Controlled by having two observers, one of each sex (1 mark)
(Total 2 marks)
Variable (ii) missing behaviour which happens simultaneously (1 mark)
Controlled by recording the ads and replaying several times (1 mark)
(Total 2 marks)
or any other sensible suggestions (2 marks) (Maximum 4 marks)

4 What does the term 'sex-role stereotyping' refer to? (2 marks)
(Options P and Q)

Answer Rigid views of character (1 mark) based on the sex of the person (1 mark) (Total 2 marks)

5 How might TV and other media communicate messages that aim to reduce sex-role stereotyping? (2 marks)
(Option Q only)

Answer Any valid suggestion: e.g. both males and females (1 mark) sharing the same task (1 mark)　　　　(Total 2 marks)
(Be careful of examples which would simply create alternative stereotypes e.g. a woman mending a plug.)

Example 7

Read this report from a local newspaper.

Simon Carruthers (26) appeared in court yesterday in connection with an incident outside The Jolly Miller pub at 11.30 p.m. on Saturday, 11th October. Carruthers, of no fixed address, is alleged to have used bad language and threatening behaviour to police when they were called by a neighbour because of the disturbance. In his defence, his solicitor claimed that he had been the victim of parental neglect in his youth, and was therefore not to be held entirely responsible for his actions. The case continues.

1 What is the name given to this particular theory? (2 marks)
(P and Q)

Answer Maternal (1 mark) deprivation (1 mark)　　　(Total 2 marks)

2 Name two other factors that might have influenced the behaviour of Simon Carruthers (2 marks)
(Option Q only)

Answer　　Media (1 mark)
　　　　　　Peers (1 mark)
　　　　　　or any other appropriate influence (1 mark)　(Maximum 2 marks)

3 According to Rutter, this explanation is unjustified. Outline the work of Rutter to show why this might be so. (4 marks)
(Option Q only)

Answer　　Correlational studies suggest:
　　(i) conflict in the home is more likely to lead to delinquency than maternal deprivation (2 marks)
　　(ii) children who lose their mothers (e.g. death) will not become delinquent if the alternative care is good (2 marks)
　　(iii) long-term damage may result from failure to form any attachments (2 marks)
　　　　　　　　(Maximum 4 marks from any combination)

Example 8

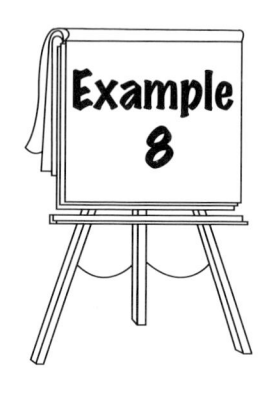

A teacher wanted to find out if a reward system would help his pupils to improve their number skills. He decided to conduct his study over two weeks with two different groups, each consisting of 10 pupils. He gave rewards such as gold stars for every correct exercise accomplished by the pupils in group A. He did not introduce any kind of reward system into group B. After the two weeks, he gave both groups the same number test. The table below shows the result of the study.

Scores on number test (maximum score 20)

Group A		Group B	
Pupil	Score	Pupil	Score
1	18	11	17
2	19	12	15
3	20	13	18
4	15	14	13
5	19	15	19
6	16	16	14
7	17	17	18
8	20	18	14
9	17	19	13
10	19	20	17

(All questions for Options P and Q)

1 How many people took part in the study? (1 mark)

Answer   20   (1 mark)

2 In this study, what is the independent variable? (1 mark)

Answer   Rewards   (1 mark)

3 What is the dependent variable? (1 mark)

Answer   Score on number test (do not accept 'the results')   (1 mark)

4 For each of the groups, calculate the mean and the range   (4 marks)

Answer   Class A   mean 18.0   (1 mark)
                           range 15-20   (1 mark)
               Class B   mean 15.8   (1 mark)
                           range 13-19   (1 mark)   (Total 4 marks)

5 From the results of the study, what conclusions can you draw about the effects of positive reinforcement? (3 marks)

Answer (i) Positive reinforcement improves number skills (1 mark)
 (ii) because the mean for A is higher than the mean for B (1 mark)
  by 2.2 (1 mark)
 (iii) 2 in A scored maximum but no one in B did (1 mark)
  (Any 3: maximum 3 marks)

6 What is meant by the term 'negative reinforcement'? (2 marks)

Answer Encouraging a certain kind of behaviour (1 mark)
  by removal of an unpleasant stimulus (1 mark) (Total 2 marks)

Example 9

The film 'Dead Poets' Society' tells the story of a brilliant but unconventional teacher, who attempts to teach his students to think for themselves and not to give in to the pressures of traditional ways of thinking. His unusual approach, and his success with his students, cause some resentment and jealousy amongst some of the other teachers, and they look for ways to get him dismissed. An incident involving the tragic death of one of his students brings circumstances to a head and provides the opportunity for his rivals to have him dismissed. One by one his students are interviewed by parents and governors of the school and persuaded to say that he misled them.

1 Name two factors involved here that make the individual students conform to group pressure. (2 marks)
(Options P and Q)

Answer Number of opponents (1 mark)
  Status of opponents (1 mark) (Total 2 marks)

2 What is the difference between compliance and conformity? (4 marks)
(Options P and Q)

Answer Compliance: going along with the group view (1 mark)
  but privately disagreeing with it (1 mark)
  Conformity: yielding to group pressure (1 mark)
  to maintain a desired relationship with the group (1 mark)
  (Total 4 marks)

3(a) From your knowledge of psychology, describe any one study in obedience
(Options P and Q)   (4 marks)

Answer   Method: basic   (1 mark)
                         accurate   (2 marks)

                              +

              Results: basic   (1 mark)
                         accurate   (2 marks)   (Maximum 4 marks)

3(b) From your knowledge of psychology, describe and evaluate any one study in obedience.   (5 marks)
(Option Q only)

Answer   Method: basic   (1 mark)
                          accurate   (2 marks)
              Results: basic   (1 mark)
                          accurate   (2 marks)
              Evaluation   (1 mark)   (Maximum 5 marks)

4(a) Name any two ethical issues which must be respected in any psychological investigation   (2 marks)
(Options P and Q)

Answer   Any appropriate issue: for example
              (i)   the right to withdraw   (1 mark)
              (ii)   anonymity   (1 mark)   (Total 2 marks)

4(b) Explain any two ethical issues which must be respected in any psychological investigation.   (4 marks)
(Option Q only)

Answer   Any appropriate issue with explanation: for example
              (i)   the right to withdraw   (1 mark)
                     because ....   (1 mark)
              (ii)   anonymity   (1 mark)
                     because ....   (1 mark)   (Maximum 4 marks)

Example 10

A police woman psychology student wanted to find out whether adults showed better behaviour at pedestrian crossing lights when they were with children than when they were alone. She stood at a pedestrian crossing lights half a mile away from a junior school for an hour on Monday 3.00-4.00 p.m. and observed adults crossing with children and without, and whether they waited for the 'green man' or whether they crossed against the 'red man'. The table below shows her results.

	Crossed on green	Crossed on red
Adults alone	ℍℍℍℍℍ (25)	ℍℍℍℍ (20)
Adults with children	ℍℍℍℍℍℍℍ𝐼𝐼 (35)	ℍ𝐼𝐼 (6)

(All questions relate to Options P and Q)

1 What is this kind of study called? (1 mark)

Answer An observation study (1 mark)

2 State a hypothesis for the study (1 mark)

Answer Adults accompanying children are more likely to cross the road according to safety regulations than if they are alone (1 mark)

3 Why did the student choose that particular time? (2 marks)

Answer Parents would probably be with children at that time (1 mark), but might not be with children at another time (1 mark) (or any appropriate answer that communicates the idea of appropriate time) (Total 2 marks)

4 From the results of this study, what conclusions can be drawn about whether or not adults pay more attention to pedestrian traffic lights when accompanied by children than when alone? (2 marks)

Answer Adults are more likely to pay attention to lights when accompanied by children (1 mark) because 35 out of 41 did with children, but only 25 out of 45 did alone (1 mark) (Total 2 marks)

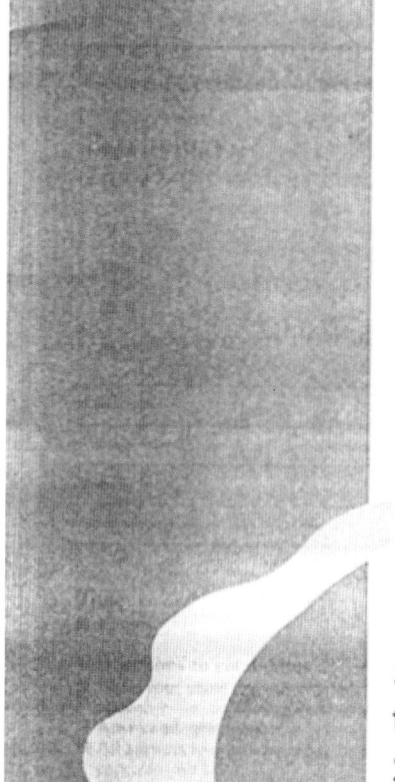

GCSE Psychology 1476

Specimen Papers for Revised 1996 Syllabus

We present here a **selection** of these specimen papers. You can obtain further sample materials and guidance from the NEAB, Manchester, M15 6EU.
Students studying for other examinations can obtain similar material from the appropriate Examining Board.

OPTION P   SECTION A   NB THIS IS A SELECTION OF QUESTIONS

- Answer **both questions.**
- You are advised to spend approximately 30 minutes on this section.
- This section carries 30 marks.

A1   A psychologist wanted to find out whether there would be a relationship between students' scores on an English test and their teacher's expectations of the scores they would obtain. From a class of 30 students, 12 were asked to volunteer to be participants. They were then given the English test and at the same time the teacher was asked to estimate the score of each participant.

The following table shows the two sets of scores.

Participant	Scores in test (Maximum score = 100)	Teacher's estimate of scores (Maximum score = 100)
A	84	75
B	75	80
C	60	55
D	45	50
E	90	80
F	20	25
G	40	45
H	50	50
I	70	65
J	60	65
K	30	25
L	20	30

(a) How many students took part in the study?

....(1)

(b) What was the aim of the study?

....
....(2)

(c) On the graph paper, plot a scattergram of the data

Title

English test scores of students

Teacher's estimate of scores

(4)

(d) What type of relationship does the graph show?

Negative correlation ☐

Positive correlation ☐

Zero correlation ☐

(Tick the correct box) (1)

(e) State an hypothesis for this study.

....
....(2)

(f) Suggest one criticism of how the study has been carried out.

....
....
....(2)

(g) Explain why this study is not an experiment

....
....
....(2)

A2 A psychologist wanted to find out if there was any difference between the number skills of men and women. She decided to conduct her study in a College of Further Education and obtained a list of names of all students. She put the names of all the male students in one hat and the names of all the female students in another hat. The flow chart shows what she did next.

```
            ┌─────────────────────────┐
            │ chose her participants by│
            │ picking 10 names out of  │
            │      each hat            │
            └─────────────────────────┘
           ↙                          ↘
┌──────────────────────┐    ┌──────────────────────────┐
│ gave the male        │    │ gave the female          │
│ participants         │    │ participants             │
│ a number test        │    │ a number test            │
└──────────────────────┘    └──────────────────────────┘
           ↘                          ↙
            ┌─────────────────────────┐
            │ collected the results of │
            │      the two tests       │
            └─────────────────────────┘
```

(a) How many people took part in this study?

....(1)

(b) Identify the sampling method used in this study.

quota sampling   ☐   (Tick the correct box)

opportunity sampling   ☐

random sampling   ☐   (1)

(c) (i) For this study what is the independent variable?

....(1)

(ii) What is the dependent variable?

....(1)

(d) The table below shows the results of the study.

Scores on number tests	
Males	Females
20	10
25	35
30	35
25	10
15	10
10	25
25	20
35	15
15	30
10	10

Use the results of the study to help you to complete the box below.

	mean	range	median
Males	21		
Females		25	17.5

(3)

(e) Identify **two** variables which the (researcher?) should have contolled when carrying out this study. Say why each should have been controlled and how each could have been controlled.

(i) Variable 1 ....

why controlled? ....
....(2)

(ii) Variable 2 ....

Why controlled? ....
....(2)

(f) What conclusions, if any, can be drawn from this study about the number skills of men and women in general? Explain your answer.

....
....
.... (4)
(Total 15)

SECTION B NB THIS IS A SELECTION OF QUESTIONS

- Answer **ALL** questions.
- You are advised to spend approximately 1 hour 30 minutes on this section
- This section carries 70 marks.

B1 Look at the diagram below and answer the questions which follow.

(a) Identify the parts labelled A-C in the diagram and complete the box below.

A	
B	
C	(3)

(b) These structures A-C help to form a sharp image. The brain uses monocular depth cues for this sharp image to make a three-dimensional picture of the world.

Name **two** monocular depth cues.

(i) ....

(ii) ....
....(2)

(c) What do psychologists mean when they say perception is an active process?
....
....
.... *(3)*

(Total 8)

B2 Read the article below and answer the questions which follow.

Pupils learn it pays to be good

Hightown is for children with emotional or behavioural difficulties who do not do well in mainstream comprehensives even though many have high IQs. It has now been selected for special praise by Her Majesty's Inspectors in a national report.

Under the Hightown scheme, children earn tokens for good behaviour, such as coming into lessons and sitting down quietly or for good work, but lose them for rudeness, laziness, disrupting lessons or violence. The tokens can be cashed in for extra swimming, football - or given tea and toast on Fridays.

Paul, ten, who has hundreds of tokens, says he tries to behave because of them. 'I was fined tokens for messing about the other week and I couldn't go to the adventure playground. They made me work instead, so I behaved the next week!'

(a) The above article illustrates

one trial learning; ☐

a token economy system; ☐

programmed learning ☐   (Tick the correct box)   *(1)*

(b) Using the terms 'conditioned response', 'primary reinforcement' and 'secondary reinforcement', explain Paul's change in behaviour.

....
....
....
....
....
....
....
....
....
.... (6)

(Total 7)

	Option P	Section A	Mark Scheme	

Response(s) to be given credit		Mark	
Question 1			
(a)	12	1	(1)
(b)	to see if there is a relationship between actual performance and teacher estimates	2	(2)
(c)	appropriate title accuracy of plotting scores on axes line of fit	1 1 1 1	(4)
(d)	positive correlation	1	(1)
(e)	statement (1) testable (1)	2	(2)
(f)	criticism (1) its effect (1)	2	(2)
(g)	no manipulated IV causing change in DV	2	(2)

(Total 15)

Response(s) to be given credit   **Mark**

Question 2

(a)   20   1   (1)

(b)   random sampling   1   (1)

(c)   IV - gender   1
        DV - scores on number test   1   (2)

(d)

25	22.5
22	

                                                                                                             (3)

(e)   any 2 appropriate variables   2 x 2
        e.g. same questions   + why?
               same amount of time + why?   (4)

(f)   result women marginally better than men (1)
        but samples size, method, task, all (2)
        encourage the researcher to be wary of
        generalising to wider population (1)   (4)

                                                                                     (Total 15)

               Option P   **Section B**   **Mark Scheme**

Response(s) to be given credit   **Mark**

Question 1

(a)   A - retina   B - cornea   C - lens   1 x   (3)

(b)   any 2   1 x   (2)

(c)   Brain has influences e.g. memory expectation etc.   1

        hypothesis/works out/calculator   1

        constructs our final experience   1   (3)

                                                                                   (Total 8)

Response(s) to be given credit	Mark	

Question 2

(a) token economy — 1 (1)

(b) correctly identify
 - conditioned response - good behaviour — 1
 - primary reinforcement - treats — 1
 - secondary reinforcement - tokens — 1
 - association - good behaviour with tokens — 1
 - tokens associated with treats — 1
 - therefore good behaviour for tokens — 1 (6)

(Total 7)

Psychology Option Q

SECTION A   NB   THIS IS A SELECTION OF QUESTIONS

- Answer ALL questions
- You are advised to spend approximately 40 minutes on this section.
- This section carries 50 marks.

A1   A psychologist wanted to find out whether there would be a relationship between students' scores on an English test and their teacher's expectations of the scores they would obtain. From a class of 30 students, 12 were asked to volunteer to be participants. They were then given the English test and at the same time the teacher was asked to estimate the score of each participant.

The following table shows the two sets of scores.

Participants	Scores in test (Maximum score = 100)	Teacher's estimate of scores (Maximum score = 100)
A	84	75
B	75	80
C	60	55
D	45	50
E	90	80
F	20	25
G	40	45
H	50	50
I	70	65
J	60	65
K	30	25
L	20	30

(a) On the graph paper, below, plot an appropriate graph for the data.

Title

(4)

(b) Identify and explain the type of relationship shown in the graph.

....
....
....*(2)*

(c) State an hypothesis for this study.

....
....
.... *(2)*

(d) Explain why this study is not an experiment.

....
....
.... (2)

(e) What conclusion, if any, can be drawn from this study?

....
....
....
.... (3)

(Total 13)

A2 A psychologist wanted to find out if there was any difference between the number skills of men and women. She decided to conduct her study in a College of Further Education and obtained a list of names of all students. She put the names of all the male students in one hat and the names of all the female students in another hat. The flow chart shows what she did next.

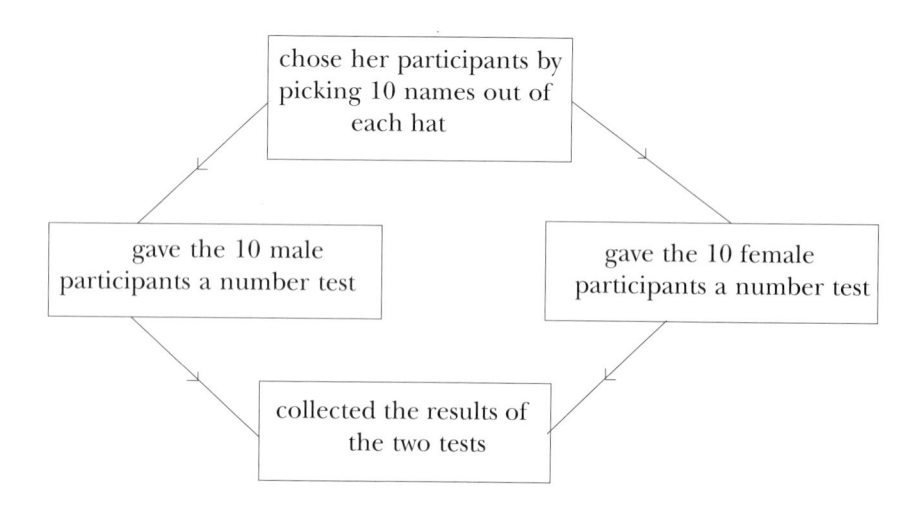

```
                    ┌────────────────────────┐
                    │ chose her participants │
                    │ by picking 10 names    │
                    │ out of each hat        │
                    └────────────────────────┘
                      ↙                    ↘
   ┌──────────────────────┐        ┌──────────────────────────┐
   │ gave the 10 male     │        │ gave the 10 female       │
   │ participants a       │        │ participants a           │
   │ number test          │        │ number test              │
   └──────────────────────┘        └──────────────────────────┘
                      ↘                    ↙
                    ┌────────────────────────┐
                    │ collected the results  │
                    │ of the two tests       │
                    └────────────────────────┘
```

(a) Identify and assess the appropriateness of the sampling method used.

....
.... (2)

(b) The table below shows the results of the study.

Table 1 Scores on a number test for males and females

Scores on number tests	
Males	Females
20	10
25	35
30	35
25	10
15	10
10	25
25	20
35	15
15	30
10	10

Complete the following summary of results using the data from Table 1.

	Mean	Median	Mode	Range
Male Participants		22.5	25	
Female Participants	22			25

(4)

(c) Apart from the control of environment variables, identify two variables which should have been controlled in this study and discuss the importance of their control.

....
....
....
.... (4)

(d) A GCSE student who saw the results drew the conclusion that the study showed women have better number skills than men.
How would you respond to this conclusion?

....
....(2)

(Total 12)

SECTION B

NB THIS IS A SELECTION OF QUESTIONS THAT APPEAR ON THE ACTUAL PAPER

- Answer ALL questions.
- You are advised to spend approximately 1 hour 50 minutes on this section.
- This section carries 85 marks.

B1 Look at the diagram below and answer the questions which follow.

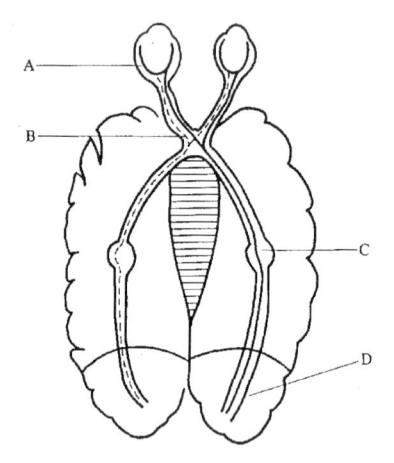

(a) Identify the parts labelled A-D in the diagram and complete the box below.

A	
B	
C	
D	

(4)

(b) Identify and describe **one** binocular depth cue used in everyday life.

....
....
.... (2)

(c) How do psychologists explain that we perceive in three dimensions yet our retinal images are in two dimensions?

....
....
....
....
....
....
....
.... *(5)*

(Total 11)

B2 Read the article below and answer the questions which follow.

Pupils learn it pays to be good

Lowfield is for children with emotional or behavioural difficulties who do not thrive in mainstream comprehensives even though many have high IQs. It has now been selected for special praise by Her Majesty's Inspectors in a national report.

Under the Lowfield scheme, children earn tokens for good behaviour, such as coming into lessons and sitting down quietly or for good work, but lose them for rudeness, laziness, disrupting lessons or violence. The tokens can be cashed in for extra swimming, football - or given tea and toast on Fridays.

Paul, ten, who has hundreds of tokens, says he tries to behave because of them. 'I was fined tokens for messing about the other week and I couldn't go to the adventure playground. They made me work instead, so I behaved the next week!'

(a) The above article illustrates

one trial learning; ☐

a token economy system; ☐   (Tick the correct box)

programmed learning. ☐   *(1)*

(b) Using the terms 'conditioned response', 'primary reinforcement' and 'secondary reinforcement', explain Paul's change in behaviour.

....
....
....
....
....
....
....
....
....
....
.... *(6)*

(c) Explain the disadvantage of trying to change Paul's behaviour in this way.

....
....
....
....
....*(3)*

(Total 10)

Option Q Section A Mark Scheme

Response(s) to be given credit   **Mark**

Question 1

(a)	graph	title	1	
		axes	1	
		plotting	1	
		line of fit	1	(4)
(b)	positive correlation		1	
	explanation		1	(2)
(c)	testable statement		2	(2)
(d)	no manipulated IV causing change in DV		2	(2)
(e)	Teacher fairly accurate in predicting student performance		1	
	recognition of limitations of study sample size/volunteers		2	(3)

(Total 13)

Response(s) to be given credit   **Mark**

Question 2

(a)   random sampling (1)   good - unbiased (1)
                                            or   2   (2)
                                poor - lack of representation (1)

(b)

21	22.5	25	25
22	22.5	10	25

                                                                            4   (4)

(c)   variable - why controlled - possible effect   2 x 2   (4)

(d)   Critical appraisal of limitations of study e.g.
        sample size, sampling method, test given   2   (2)

                                                                                  (Total 12)

Option Q   Section B   Mark Scheme

Response(s)   given credit   **Mark**

Question 1

(a)   A - Retina   1
        B - Optical chiasma   1
        C - L.G.N. (Lateral geniculate nucleus)   1
        D - Visual cortex   1   (4)

(b)   convergence, retinal disparity   2   (2)

(c)   retinal images are flat (2D)   1
        perception is interpretation   1
        (brain converts, translation, organisation, etc.)   1
        using cues or hypothesis/schemata   5 x 1   1
        leading to 3D model (implied)   1
        perception 'active process'   1
        related to e.g. Muller-Lyer, Gestalt, constancies)   1
        past experience mentioned   1   (5)
                            (any of the above)
                                                                             (Total 11)

Response(s) to be given credit	**Mark**	
(a) token economy	1	(1)
(b) correctly identify		
- conditioned response - good behaviour	1	
- primary reinforcement - treats	1	
- secondary reinforcement - tokens	1	
- association - good behaviour with tokens	1	
- tokens associated with treats	1	
- therefore good behaviour for tokens	1	(6)
(c) Only producing good behaviour for tokens/treats	1	
no guarantee his behaviour will continue without tokens	1	
& good behaviour pleasant in itself (intrinsic worth) (or other)	1	(3)
	(Total 10)	

Index

A* grade, 3
Adorno, T., 161, 163
adrenaline (*see also* noradreline), 86
affectionless psychopathy, 140, 143
aggression, 56, 57
aggression-frustration hypothesis, 56
'Aha!' experience, 55
Ahrens, S.R., 138
Ainsworth, M., 138, 139, 143
alertness, kinds of, 119-120
Allport, G.Q., 114, 161, 167, 170
altruism, 168, 170
amnesia, 71, 73
   retograde and anterograde, 71
androgyny, 148-150
animals and language, 98-9
animal deprivation studies, 35
Annis, R.C. and Frost, B., 25
arousal, 79, 85-6, 90, 113
artifical intelligence, 81, 98, 100, 106 108, 119
Asch, S.E., 153, 155, 156, 176, 178
Aschoff, J., 121
assessment objectives, 5
assimilation and accommodation, 127, 132
Atkinson, R.C. and Shiffrin, R.M., 64, 66
attachment and separation, 137-145
attachment, theories of, 139-141, 143
attachments, development of, 137-9, 142
attention, 112-8
   different kinds of, 120, 123
   factors influencing, 112-3
   ways of studying it, 113-4, 116
attribution theory, 153, 156
attributional bias, 155
avoidance learning, 47, 49
audience effects, 166-7, 170
authoritarian personality, 161
autonomic nervous system, 78, 85, 90

Bandura, A., 54, 57, 140, 148
Bartlett, F., 63, 64, 65-6
behaviourism, 41-2, 48
behaviourist approaches to learning theory, 41-53
Bem, S., 148,
Bernstein, B., 95, 100

Binet, A., 106, 108
binocular depth cues, 24, 25, 28
biofeedback, 87, 90, 122-4
biological approaches to socialisation, 147, 149-50
biological factors in socialisation, 146-7, 149
biosocial approach to socialisation, 147, 149-50
Blakemore, C. and Cooper, J., 35, 37
Boden, M., 105
bonding, 57, 139, 141
Bower, T., 37
Bowlby, J., 89, 131, 140-1, 142, 143
Brady, J., 86
brain damage and disease, 71, 73
brain, structure of, 79, 81
brain, ways of studying it, 80, 82
Broadbent, D., 114, 116
Brown, G., 98, 100
Bruner, J., 62, 65, 96, 97, 100, 128, 132
Bruner, J. and Minturn, A., 27, 31
Bryan, J. and Test, T., 168
bystander apathy, 167
bystander intervention, 167-8
   factors involved in, 167-8, 170

Calhoun, J.B., 56
Cannon, W., 86
Cannon-Bard theory, 88, 90
carpentered environment, 25, 36
Carmichael, L., 64, 66, 71
cataract patient studies, 35, 37
central character traits, 153, 155
central nervous system, 77-8
central processor, 115
cerebrum, structure of, 79, 81
Cherry, E.C., 114
child-minding, 131-2
chimpanzees and language, 99
Chomsky, N., 97-9, 100
circadian rhythms, 121, 123
classical conditioning, 42-5
closure, principle of, 27
co-action effect, 167, 170
cognitive approaches to learning theory, 54-5, 57
cognitive dissonance, 160, 162
cognitive map, 55, 57
comparative psychology, 41-2, 48
compliance, 175-6
communication in animals, 99-100
communication use of language, 98, 100
competence and performance, 98, 99
concept formation, 107, 108
conformity, 175-6
connector neurones, 78,
consciousness, 119
consciousness, control of, 122

constancy, 24, 25, 28
context-dependent learning, 71, 73
convergence, 25
convergent and divergent thinking, 105
 (*see also* thinking)
coursework requirements, 13
Craik, I. and Lockhart, R., 64, 66, 72
Crick, F. and Mitchison, G., 72, 122-3
cross-cultural studies, 36, 37, 148
crying in babies, 138
cues (*see* mnemonics)

2-D images and 3-D percepts, 22, 23, 28
de Bono, E., 105, 108
decay in memory, 71, 73
defining the situation, 168, 170
de-individuation, 169
Dement, W., 120
Dement, W., and Wolpert, E., 121
Deutsch, D. and Collins, J., 161, 163
Deutsch, D. and Deutsch, J., 114, 116
deviance, 177-8
de Villiers, J. and P., 98, 100
dialect, 95
diffusion of responsibility, 167, 170
discrimination, 44, 49, 160, 162
displacement, 161
dispositional attribution, 153, 155, 156
Dollard, J., 161
dominant response, 167, 170
Donaldson, M., 128, 132
dreaming, function of, 119-126
dreamwork, 121-3
dual task techniques, 113-4, 116

Ebbinghaus, H., 63, 64, 66
ego, 121, 130, 140
Ekman, P., 87
elaborated and restricted codes of speech, 95, 100
Electra complex, 140, 148-9
Emerson, J., 138
emotion, arousal and stress, 85-93
emotion
 as perceptual set, 28, 113
 physiological correlates, 85-6, 90
 physiological foundations, 77-84
 theories of, 87-8, 90
emotions, acquisition of, 89, 90
empiricism, 17, 18-9, 34
enactive representation
 (*see* modes of representation)
encoding in memory, 61-5
environmentalist, 18
environmental factors, 18, 25, 65, 85, 87, 112
Erikson, E., 28

escape learning, 47, 49
ethical issues, 93, 99, 199, 175, 177-8
ethnocentrism, 161
ethological approaches to learning theory, 55-6
eugenics, 106
examiners' report, 4
expectations in perceptual set, 28, 113
extinction, 44
eye contact, 138
Eysenck, H., 105, 107
Eysenck, H. and Jensen, A., 106
Eysenck, H. and Keanes, M., 106, 114

Fantz, R., 36, 37, 138
fear of strangers, 138, 142
Festinger, L., 160, 162
'fight or flight', 78, 86, 90
figure-ground, 26
filter models of attention, 114-5
 challenges to, 115-6
fixed action patterns, 55-6
focal attention, 120, 123
forgetting, factors affecting it, 70-1, 72-3
 theories of, 64, 71-2
Fraenkle-Brunswick, E., 161,
Fraiberg, J., 138
Freud, A., 141, 143
Freud, S., 71-3, 105, 121, 123, 130, 139-40, 148-9, 161, 163
Friedman, H. and Rosenman, R., 87
frustration-aggression hypothesis, 161
F-scale, 161
functional fixedness, 106
fundamental attribution error, 155

Galton, F., 106, 108
galvanic skin response, 87
Gardner, H., 105, 107
Gazzaniga, M., 80, 82
gender and socialisation, 146-152
gender role, 147-9
General Adaptation Syndrome, 86-7
generalisation, 44-9
generalisation gradient, 44
genetic inheritance, 89, 90, 149
genetic transmission, 18, 106
Gesell, A., 18, 20
Gestalt psychologists, 26, 105, 106
Gibson, E., 28
Gibson, E. and Walk, R., 36-7
Gilchrist, J. and Nesberg, L., 27, 31
Golombok, S., 149
Gooch, S., 80, 82
Goodenough, S., 121
gradient of texture, 24
Gregory, R., 28, 35, 37

group norms, 175-6, 177-8
group pressures, 175-181

habituation, 120, 123
halo effect, 153, 160
Harlow, H., 54-5, 57, 106, 108, 138, 140-3
Hearne, K., 121
Hebb, D., 18, 20
height in plane, 24
Held, R. and Heim, A., 35, 37
Hess, E., 34-5, 37
Hofling, C., 177-8
Holms, D. and Rahe, R., 87
hormones, 147
Hubel, D. and Wiesel, T., 35, 37
Hudson, L., 36-7, 105, 108
Hughes, M., 128, 132
human development issues, 22
hypnosis, 122, 124
hypothalamus, 79, 81

iconic representation
 (*see* modes of representation)
id, 121, 130, 140
identifying with the aggressor, 140, 148
imagery (*see* mnemonic systems)
imaging, 87, 90, 123
implicit personality theories, 153, 155, 159
implosion therapy, 87, 90
imprinting, 56-7, 139
in-groups and out-groups, 160
IQ tests, 106, 107-8
insight learning, 55, 105
instrumental conditioning, 45
intellectual development (Piaget), 127-136
interactionism, 17, 18-20
intelligence, 104-111
 definitions of, 104-5, 107-8
 its acquisition, 106
interference, 71, 73
 proactive and retroactive, 71-2
introspection, 113

James-Lange theory, 87-8, 90
jetlag effects, 121, 123
Jones, E., 27
Jung, C.G., 121, 123

Kahnemann, D., 115-6
Kelley, H., 153, 155-6
Kelman, H., 176, 178
key word method, 63, 65
kitten carousel, 35

Kitty Genovese murder, 167
Klaus, R., 138
Klein, M., 121
Kohlberg, L., 129, 130-1
Köhler, W., 34, 37, 54, 55, 57, 105, 108

Labov, W., 95, 100
Language Acquisition Device, 97
language development, 96-8, 100
 theories of, 96, 100
language,
 its nature, acquisition and use, 94-103
 structure of, 94
 and thinking, 94-6, 100
 use of, 98, 100
La Piere, R., 160
Latané, B. and Darley, J., 167-8
Latané, B. and Rodin, J., 167
latent learning, 54
lateral thinking, 105-8 (*see also* thinking)
Law of Effect, 45
Law of Exercise, 45
Laws of Prägnanz (Principles of Organisation), 26, 28
learned helplessness, 89, 90
learning, behaviourist approaches, 41-53
 cognitive and ethological approaches, 54-60
learning sets (learning how to learn), 55, 57, 106, 108
levels of processing model, 64, 65-6, 72
Levine, J., 86, 89
limbic system, 79, 81
linguistic relativity hypothesis, 95, 100
Linton, J., 169, 171
Loftus, E. and Loftus, G., 64, 66
Lorenz, K., 56, 57
Luchins, A., 106, 108, 153, 156
lucid dreams, 121

Marr, D., 28
maternal deprivation, 89, 90, 140, 143
maturation, 17,
McGarrigle, J. and Donaldson, M., 128, 132
meditation, 87, 90, 122-4
memory - how does it work?, 61-9
method of loci, 62, 65
Miles, L., 121
Milgram, S., 177-8
mnemonic systems, 62-3, 65, 71, 73
modelling, 55, 87, 168, 170
models of attention, 114-5
models of thinking, 106, 108
modes of representation (Bruner), 62, 65, 97, 128, 132
Money, J. and Ehrhardt, A., 147
monocular depth cues, 24-5, 28

monotropy theory, 140, 143
moral development, 127-136
Moray, N., 114
motivated forgetting, 71, 73
motivation, 27, 85, 113, 116
motor neurones, 78
Müller-Lyer illusion, 31, 36
multiple intelligences, 105, 107
multi-store model, 63-4, 65-6
Myers, D., 80, 82

National Curriculum, 1
nativism, 17, 18-20, 34
nativist views, 34
nature-nurture debate, 17, 20-1
  in intelligence, 106, 108
  in language, 94, 103
  in perception, 33-40
'naughty Teddy', 128
NEAB new syllabus, 1-13
Necker cube, 26
negative reinforcement, 47, 49
Neisser, U., 115-6
neonate (infant) studies, 36-7
nerve cells (neurones), 78
nervous system, 77-8, 81
neurotransmitters, 78
noradrenaline, 78
Norman, D., 115-6
NREM sleep, 120-123

obedience, 175-6
  factors involved, 177
  studies in, 177
observational learning theory, 55
Oedipus complex, 140, 143, 148-9
one-trial learning, 44, 49
operant conditioning, 45, 49
Options P and Q, 5, 6-13
organisation in memory, 64, 71, 73
Ornstein, R., 80, 82
Osgood, C., 105
Overton, D., 70

parasympathetic division, 78, 86
parent-child interaction, 137-9, 140-2
parenting, 130-2, 141-2
Pavlov, I., 42, 44, 48
peg word method, 63, 65
perception, 22-32, 112
  factors affecting, 27
  the nature-nurture debate in, 33-40
perceptual adaptation studies, 34, 37

perceptual defence, 28
perceptual set, 27, 28, 112-3, 116
peripheral attention, 120, 123
peripheral nervous system, 77-8
Perrin, S. and Spencer, C., 176, 178
personality type, 87, 89, 93
Pettigrew, J., 160, 163
phasic alertness, 120, 123
Piaget, J., 95-7, 100, 105, 107-8, 127-9, 130-2, 142
Piliavin, I., 168
play, 95, 131-2
positive marking, 4
positive and negative reinforcement, 47
Postman, L., Bruner, J. and McGuiness, J., 28
preferred adult, 138, 142
prejudice, 159, 162
  foundations of, 160, 163
  positive and negative, 160
  overcoming it, 161, 160
pre-school provision, 131-2
presence of other people, 167, 170
primacy effect, 27, 113, 116,153, 156
primary and secondary reinforcement, 46, 49
'prison' experiment, 169
problem solving, 104-111
proximity, principle of, 26
psychoanalytical approach, 139-40, 143, 146, 148-50
psychosexual stages, 139-40, 143, 146, 148-50
punishment, 47, 49

Raugh, M. and Atkinson, R., 63, 65, 71
recency effect, 113, 153, 156
Recent Life Experience Scale, 87
reinforcement, 45-9
REM sleep, 120-1, 123
remembering, processes involved in, 61-6
remembering and forgetting, 70-6
repression, 71
reticular activating system (RAS), 79, 81
retrieval in memory, 61, 64-5
Riesen, A., 35, 37
role expecation, 169
role groupings, 169
role of family, 130
role of parents, 137
Rosenthal, R., 95
Rubin's vase, 26
Rutter, M., 140-3

Sapir, E. and Whorf, B., 95, 100
'S.B.', 35
Schachter, S. and Singer, J., 88-90
schedules of reinforcement, 46, 49
schemata, 107-8, 127

Sears, R., 148
Secord, P. and Blackman, C., 162-3
Segall, M., Campbell, H. and Herskowitz, J., 36-7
self-consciousness, 119, 123
self-fulfilling prophecy, 95, 169, 171
Seligman, M., 89
Selye, H., 86
sensation and perception, 23, 33
sensory neurones, 78
serial position effect, 71, 73
sex-identity, 148-9
shadowing, 113-4, 116
Shaffer, D., 114, 138
shape constancy, 37
shaping behaviour, 45
Sherif, M., 162-3
Shields, J., 106
short and long-term memory, 63-5
single channel models (*see* filter models)
situational attribution, 154-6
Skodak, M. and Skeels, H., 106
Skinner, B.F., 45, 49, 96, 100
sleep, 119-126
   physiological correlates, 120
Smith, C. and Lloyd, B., 148
Snow, C., 98, 100
sociability in children, 135, 142
socialisation, 137-8, 142-3
social facilitation, 166-7
social influence, 166-174
social learning approach, 140, 146, 148-50
social norms, 137, 168, 171, 175
social perception, 153-8
social role, 146
Solley, C. and Haigh, J., 28, 32
Solomon, G., 86
somatic nervous system, 78
Sperry, R., 80, 82
states of consciousness, 119-126
stages of cognitive development (Piaget), 128, 132
stages of moral development (Freud), 130, 132
   (Kohlberg), 129, 132
   (Piaget), 129, 132
state dependent learning, 70-1, 73
stereotyping and prejudice, 159-165
stimulus-response approaches, 42-9, 96, 99
strange situation, 139
Stratton, G., 34, 37
stress, 85-7
   causes of, 87, 89, 90
   treatments for, 87, 90
styles of child-minding/leadership, 130
super-ego, 130, 140
symbolic archetypes, 121
symbolic representation, 62, 65
sympathetic division, 78, 86
synaptic transmission, 78

territoriality, 56-7
thalamus, 79, 81
thinking, 104-111
   definitions of, 104-5
   theories of, 105-6, 108
Thorndike, E., 45, 49, 105, 108
Tinbergen, N., 56-7
Tolman, E., 54-5, 57
tonic alertness, 120, 123
Triesman, A., 114, 116
Triplett, N., 166
Tulving, E. and Pearlstone, Z., 64, 66, 71
Turnbull, C., 36-7
Type A and Type B persons, 87, 93

Valins, S. and Hohmans, G., 88
values in perceptual set, 28, 113, 116
verbal behaviour, 96
violence in inner cities, 65
   on TV, 55
visual cliff, 36
Von Senden, M., 35, 37
Vygotsky, L., 96-7, 100

'War of the Ghosts' (Bartlett), 63-4, 66
Watson, J.B., 18, 19, 89, 95, 100
Webb, W., 121
Webb, W. and Kersey, J., 121
Weiss, J., 86
Wundt, W., 113

Yerkes-Dodson Law, 86, 90, 93, 167

Zajonc, R., 167, 170
Zimbardo, P., 167, 170